SpringerBriefs in Computer Science

SpringerBriefs present concise summaries of cutting-edge research and practical applications across a wide spectrum of fields. Featuring compact volumes of 50 to 125 pages, the series covers a range of content from professional to academic. Typical topics might include:

- A timely report of state-of-the art analytical techniques
- A bridge between new research results, as published in journal articles, and a contextual literature review
- A snapshot of a hot or emerging topic
- An in-depth case study or clinical example
- A presentation of core concepts that students must understand in order to make independent contributions

Briefs allow authors to present their ideas and readers to absorb them with minimal time investment. Briefs will be published as part of Springer's eBook collection, with millions of users worldwide. In addition, Briefs will be available for individual print and electronic purchase. Briefs are characterized by fast, global electronic dissemination, standard publishing contracts, easy-to-use manuscript preparation and formatting guidelines, and expedited production schedules. We aim for publication 8–12 weeks after acceptance. Both solicited and unsolicited manuscripts are considered for publication in this series.

**Indexing: This series is indexed in Scopus, Ei-Compendex, and zbMATH **

Aswani Kumar Cherukuri • Sumaiya Thaseen Ikram
Gang Li • Xiao Liu

Encrypted Network Traffic Analysis

 Springer

Aswani Kumar Cherukuri
Vellore Institute of Technology
Vellore, Tamil Nadu, India

Gang Li
Deakin University
Burwood, NSW, Australia

Sumaiya Thaseen Ikram
Vellore Institute of Technology
Vellore, Tamil Nadu, India

Xiao Liu
Deakin University
Burwood, NSW, Australia

ISSN 2191-5768 ISSN 2191-5776 (electronic)
SpringerBriefs in Computer Science
ISBN 978-3-031-62908-2 ISBN 978-3-031-62909-9 (eBook)
https://doi.org/10.1007/978-3-031-62909-9

This Springer imprint is published by the registered company Springer Nature Switzerland AG
The registered company address is: Gewerbestrasse 11, 6330 Cham, Switzerland

If disposing of this product, please recycle the paper.

Foreword

Encryption, while essential for protecting data privacy and security, also poses significant challenges. In an era where data breaches and cyber threats are escalating in both frequency and sophistication, the analysis of encrypted network traffic is essential for maintaining cybersecurity. "Encrypted Network Traffic Analysis" by Aswani Kumar Cherukuri, Sumaiya Thaseen, Gang Li, and Xiao Liu is a crucial resource for understanding and tackling this complex domain. I have closely followed the work of these esteemed authors, whose contributions and deep expertise in network security, machine learning, and data analytics are highly regarded within both academic and professional circles.

As encryption becomes ubiquitous, analysing encrypted traffic without compromising privacy is a paramount challenge. This book addresses these challenges, providing a comprehensive guide to various methodologies employed in the field. The text begins by explaining the significance of encrypted network traffic analysis in modern Internet infrastructure. Then, the authors have provided a solid foundation for the principles of encrypted network traffic analysis. One of the book's core strengths lies in its detailed examination of statistical and machine learning techniques for encrypted traffic analysis. From supervised and unsupervised learning algorithms to advanced deep learning models, the authors meticulously describe how these techniques can be applied to detect anomalies, classify traffic, and infer patterns in encrypted data. The inclusion of real-world datasets and practical tools further enhances the utility of this book, making it a valuable reference for both academia and industry.

The industrial applications of encrypted network traffic analysis are vast and varied. From enhancing intrusion detection systems and improving network performance to ensuring regulatory compliance and safeguarding sensitive data, the techniques discussed in this book have far-reaching implications. The authors provide detailed explanations of how these techniques can be deployed in real-world scenarios, offering readers a practical roadmap for implementation.

"Encrypted Network Traffic Analysis" is a comprehensive guide that equips its readers with the knowledge and tools necessary to navigate the complexities of encrypted traffic analysis. For students, this book offers a thorough introduction to the field. Researchers will find a wealth of information on the latest techniques, datasets, and tools, while practitioners will appreciate the actionable insights and detailed guidance on deploying these techniques in real-world environments.

I strongly encourage you to explore the depths of this book and apply its insights to your work. The knowledge contained within these pages is essential for advancing the field of network security and for protecting our digital infrastructure in an increasingly encrypted world. I sincerely congratulate the authors and the publisher for their efforts in bringing out this book.

Sincerely,

2025 President, IEEE Computer Society,   Hironori Washizaki
Professor and Associate Dean of Research
Promotion Division
Waseda University
Shinjuku, Japan

Preface

It is estimated that more than 95% of internet traffic is encrypted. This encrypted network traffic ensures privacy, confidentiality and integrity of the communications. Further, it also protects against various cyberattacks. However, this significant increase in encrypted network traffic is also transforming the threat landscape and introducing new attack vectors. There are raising concerns over the potential cyber-attacks that are concealed under encrypted network communications and malicious payloads in encrypted traffic. Many organizations across the globe have recognised the need to inspect and analyse encrypted communications and traffic. Classical network traffic analysis techniques such as Deep Packet Inspection (DPI) fail to analyse, classify and detect anomalies in the encrypted network traffic. Decrypting the encrypted traffic, both inbound and outbound, is one of the possible solutions. However, there are concerns about this approach, which include compromise in the privacy of the communications, performance-related issues, etc. There are methods in the literature that analyse the unencrypted details in the packet header. Similarly, there are methods that analyse the traffic flows and understand the network traffic patterns to derive inferences about the traffic. However, these methods depend on network traffic flows and telemetry of the traffic. These methods suffer from a high false positive rate. Researchers are exploring intelligent techniques that can inspect, analyse and classify the encrypted network traffic to detect anomalies. These techniques would be useful to network administrators, law enforcement agencies, etc., to identify different kinds of encrypted traffic in the network and thereby inspect anomalies in the traffic. In the recent past, there have been efforts in the literature to adopt machine learning and deep learning–based approaches to address the above problem.

This book provides a detailed study of the sources of encrypted network traffic, methods and techniques for analysing, classifying and detecting the encrypted traffic. While discussing the state of the art, we also provide some of our research findings on implementing intelligent techniques for this task. The objectives of this volume is:

- To discuss the encrypted network traffic, protocols and applications of the encrypted network traffic
- To analyse the challenges and issues with encrypted network traffic
- To systematically introduce the analysis and classification of encrypted traffic and methods in detecting the anomalies in encrypted traffic
- To study the effect of traditional approaches of encrypted traffic such as deep packet inspection and flow based approaches on various encrypted traffic applications for identifying attacks
- To discuss intelligent techniques for analysing the encrypted network traffic with case studies

The above objectives are addressed in five chapters of this book. Chapter 1 provides fundamentals of network traffic analysis, anomalies in network traffic and protocols for encrypted network traffic. Chapter 2 provides an overview of the challenges and issues with encrypted network traffic and the new threat vectors introduced by encrypted network traffic. Chapter 3 provides details on the analysis of encrypted network traffic and the classification of various kinds of encrypted network traffic. Chapter 4 discusses techniques for detecting attacks against encrypted protocols. Chapter 5 analyses AI-based approaches for anomaly detection. We believe that this book provides a comprehensive coverage of the topic, resources for a deeper understanding and pointers for future research. Hence, it would serve students, researchers and industry practitioners as a valuable reference work.

We sincerely acknowledge the research grant (SPARC/2018-19/P616/SL) from the Ministry of Human Resource Development (MHRD), Govt. of India, under the Scheme for Promotion of Academic and Research Collaboration (SPARC) programme.

Vellore, Tamil Nadu, India   Aswani Kumar Cherukuri
                                                                  Sumaiya Thaseen Ikram
Burwood, NSW, Australia   Gang Li
                                                                            Xiao Liu

Acknowledgements

We express our sincere gratitude to Ministry of Human Resource Development (MHRD), Govt. of India, for the research grant (SPARC/2018-19/P616/SL) under the Scheme for Promotion of Academic and Research Collaboration (SPARC). This book is one of the outcome of the research efforts carried out under this grant. We also sincerely thank Dr. Hironori Washizaki for providing foreword for this book in spite of his busy schedule. This collaborative effort would not have been possible without the support and expertise of our colleagues, research scholars, and students. We thank our family members for their constant support, understanding, and encouragement.

Aswani Kumar Cherukuri and Sumaiya Thaseen express gratitude to the Vellore Institute of Technology, Vellore, India, for the extensive support in executing the research project and also for the encouragement toward international research collaborations.

Special thanks to the Springer editorial and publishing team for their support and untiring efforts in bringing out this book.

Contents

Chapter 1
Introduction

1.1 Security in TCP/IP

Internet is regarded as a network of a series of backbone networks operated by Internet Service Providers (ISP), Wide Area Networks (WAN), Local Area Networks (LAN) and the devices that connect them. Cryptographic techniques provide security services in the TCP/IP protocol stack. These services include confidentiality, integrity, authentication and digital signatures. Traditional network monitoring systems such as firewalls and intrusion detection systems (IDS) analyse the network traffic by inspecting the individual packets or the session flows during the communication. Cryptographic techniques are generally deployed in the TCP/IP protocol stack to secure Internet communications [1]. This deployment provides various security services, including confidentiality, integrity, authentication and digital signatures in both client and server applications. In general, security is implemented at the top three layers of TCP/IP protocol stack, i.e. application layer, transport layer and network layer. Though security is considered at the application layer, not all the applications are secured here. Hence the security implementations are also either at the transport or network layers. Figure 1.1 shows the implementation of security at TCP/IP layers. In the following sections, we discuss the security implementations in the network, transport and application layers.

1.2 Security at the Network Layer

Security at the network layer is achieved through a collection of protocols called IP Security (IPSec) designed by the Internet Engineering Task Force (IETF). For application layer data, the transport layer header user datagram protocol and internet control message protocol (TCP/UDP/ICMP) User Datagram Protocol and Internet

© The Author(s), under exclusive license to Springer Nature Switzerland AG 2024
A. K. Cherukuri et al., *Encrypted Network Traffic Analysis*, SpringerBriefs in Computer Science, https://doi.org/10.1007/978-3-031-62909-9_1

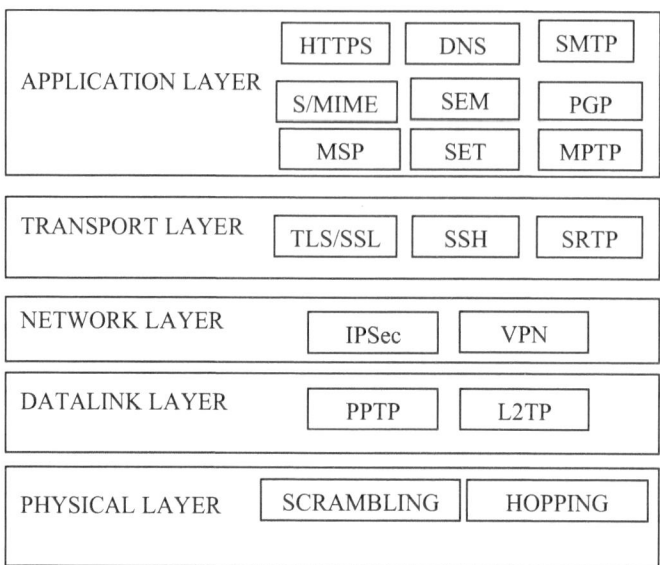

Fig. 1.1 TCP/IP protocol suite with security considerations

Control Message Protocol) is added at the transport layer. These details serve as a payload to the IP at the network layer. Subsequently, an IP header is added to this payload. IPSec operates in two modes: transport mode and tunnel mode. Figures 1.2a and 1.2b shows the IPSec operation in both modes. In transport mode, IPSec protects the payload from the transport layer and does not protect the IP header details of the payload. When IPSec is implemented in transport mode, an IPSec header is appended between the original IP header and the IP payload. This mode is implemented in the end-to-end communications to provide encryption and authentication. In tunnel mode of IPSec implementation, the original IP header is encapsulated with IP payload. Then IPSec header is inserted between the new IP header and encapsulated IP payload. Due to this, IPSec also protects the payload and original IP header. Tunnel mode is implemented between routers, between a router and a host or between a host and a router. IPSec provides security services such as confidentiality through encryption. It uses symmetric and asymmetric encryption algorithms for encryption and key exchange.

Further, it uses Internet Key Exchange (IKE) for mutual authentication and key establishment. Processing and security implementation of inbound and outbound packets at a router or at a node are governed by the security policy database and security association database [2]. The following figures illustrate the security implementation at the network layer through IPSec in transport and tunnel modes. New IP header contains information about the routing, including the source and destination address of IPSec gateways. IPSec implementation with encapsulating security payload achieves confidentiality, integrity and authentication. In the transport mode, the original IP header is used and a new IP header is created in the tunnel mode. Hence the internal routing information is protected, providing limited traffic flow and confidentiality of the payload, authentication and integrity. Different encrypted

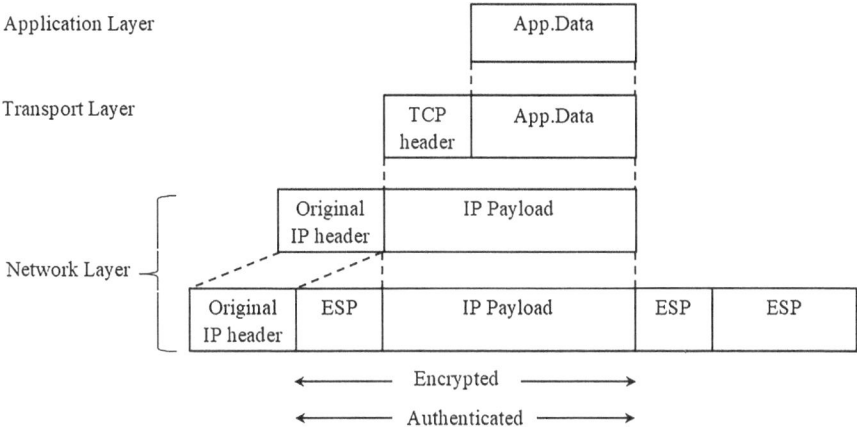

Fig. 1.2a IPSec operation in transport mode

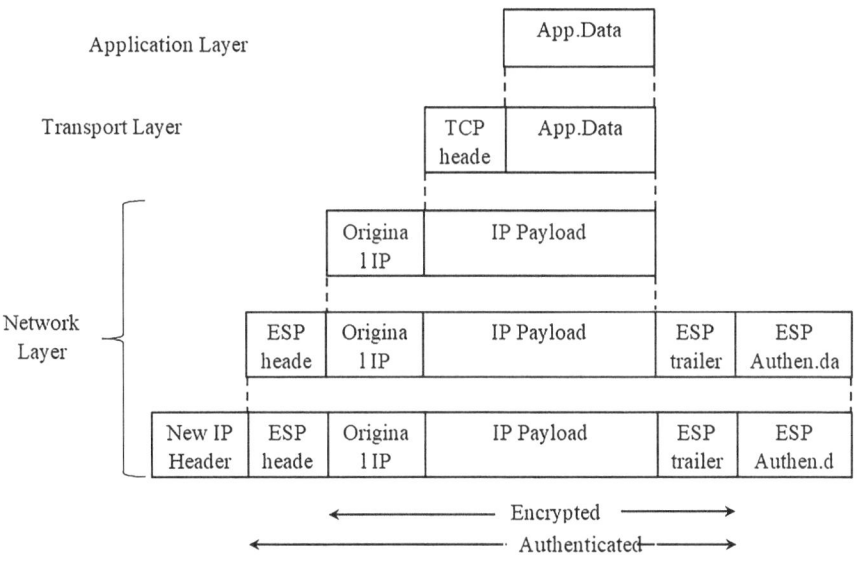

Fig. 1.2b IPSec operation in tunnel mode

parameters and unencrypted parameters of IPSec in transport and tunnel modes are given in Tables 1.1 and 1.2.

Figure 1.3 shows a packet capture of ESP traffic when communicating with a Virtual Private Network (VPN) contractor from a local client. The top panel of the Wireshark shows the sequence of packets filtered using ESP protocol. The middle panel shows a detailed layered view of every single packet captured. The source address, destination address, source port, destination port, length and checksum are visible in the network layered view. As the packets are encapsulated, the SPI and ESP sequence numbers are also shown for every packet. The bottom view shows the hexadecimal representation of the packet capture.

Table 1.1 IPSec encrypted parameters in transport and tunnel modes

Parameters of IPSec		
Original IP header	Source IP address	Address of source IP
	Destination IP address	Address of destination IP
	TOS-type of service	Information about the path of packets traverse across the network
	Protocol	Information about transport layer protocol
	TTL	Total time of packet exists in the network
	Fields help to route the packets: Identification	Split large messages in IP packets Information about all the fragments of a packet
	Flags	Used to control and identify fragments
	Fragmentation offset fields	Helps to bring original packet by keeping the fragments in order
AH/ESP Authentication Header and Encapsulation Security Payload header	Depends on value of IP protocol field: authentication header (AH) = 51 or ESP = 50 encapsulation security payload (ESP) header:	It includes information about TCP, UDP, ICMP:
	Security parameter index (SPI)	Destination address and protocol from IP header
	Sequence number	Provides anti-replay protection
	Payload data	Original data with TCP header
	AH header Next header	Indicates value of upper layer protocol
	Payload length	Length of the header
	Reserved	Not used. Set to zeroes
	SPI	Destination address and protocol from IP header
	Sequence number	Provides anti-replay protection
	Authenticated data	Payload plus IP header gets authenticated
IP payload	It contains information about the original IP packet or data along with IV—Initialisation vector	Prevents repetition in data encryption
	TCP header information: Source port	Source port number
	Destination port	Destination port number
	Sequence number	Gives information like counter about number of bytes sent outward by a host
	Header length	Size of TCP header
	Flags	Gives information about particular connection state
	Window size	Maximum size of data sender can transmit before receiver's acknowledgement
	TCP checksum	Checking error in data and header

(continued)

Table 1.1   (continued)

Parameters of IPSec

ESP trailer	Padding	Checks the encrypted payload are in exact multiples of block size
	Pad length	Used to show the length in bytes of padding fields
	Next header	Used to identify whether the payload is TCP/UDP/ICMP For transport mode, ESP trailer next header value = 6(IPv4) or 60(IPv6) Tunnel mode, ESP trailer next header value = 4(IPv4) or 41(IPv6)
ESP authentication data	The entire transport layer segment plus ESP trailer gets encrypted	Information about all the cipher text along with ESP header
New IP header	Source and destination addresses of two IPSec gateways	It contains information about the routing

Table 1.2   IPSec unencrypted parameters in transport and tunnel modes

Unencrypted parameters

IPSec modes	Fields	Parameters	Variables used in Wireshark
Transport mode	Original IP header	Source IP address Destination IP address Source port Destination port Protocol TOS TTL Input logical interface	ip.src ip.dst src.port dst.port ip.proto ip.tos ip.ttl
	ESP trailer	Padding Pad length Next header fields	esp.pad esp.pad_len esp.protocol
Tunnel mode	New IP header	Source and destination addresses of two IPSec gateways	
Transport and tunnel modes	ESP authentication	Integrity check values (ICV)	esp.icv
	IP payload	Initialisation vector (IV)	esp.iv
	ESP header	SPI Sequence number	esp.spi esp.sequence (or) esp.sequence-analysis. expected-sn

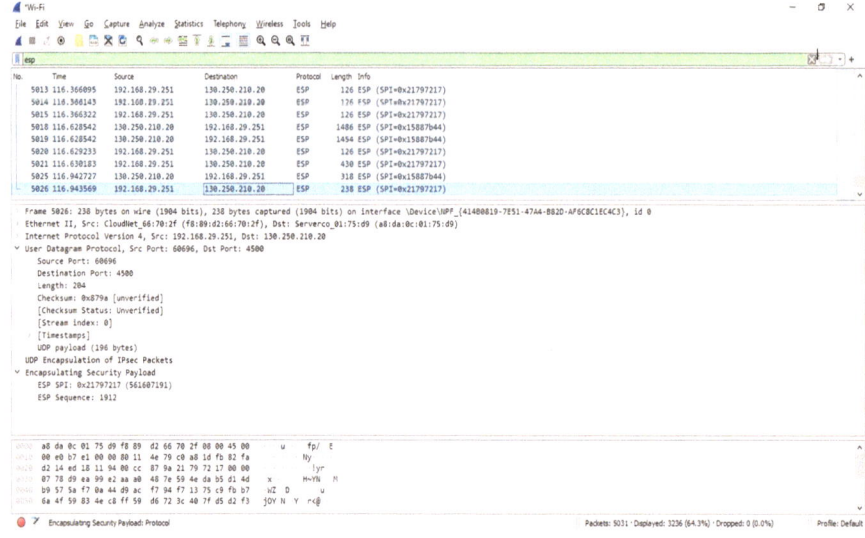

Fig. 1.3 VPN traffic in tunnel mode

1.3   Security at Transport Layer

The Transport Layer Security (TLS) protocol stack achieves security at the transport layer. Applications in the upper layer use the security services offered by the TLS at the transport layer. Specifically, the TLS protocol suite is located between the application and transport layers. Hence the application data from the upper layer is fragmented, compressed (optional) and then signed through a Message Authentication Code (MAC). Subsequently, the compressed message and its MAC code are encrypted. TLS protocol stack has handshake protocol, cipher spec protocol, the alert protocol, heartbeat protocol and record protocol.

Handshake protocol negotiates the security parameters and encryption keys with the other communication node. Further, it authenticates the communicating nodes to each other. Then the record protocol uses other protocols and security primitives established by the handshake protocol and carries the secured payload to the transport layer protocol, i.e. TCP. While transmitting the payload, the record protocol achieves confidentiality and message authentication through encryption and hash algorithms. Then the TLS headers are appended to the encrypted payload and transferred to the transport layer. TLS uses both TCP and UDP. Datagram TLS is mainly meant for VPN applications. TLS establishes a secured logical tunnel between the client (browser) and the server (destination node). An organisation or a client gets a digital certificate from a vendor. An employee of the organisation accesses a web server through TLS. Then the client and the server exchange their digital certificates and relevant other parameters such that the rest of the communication is secured through encryption.

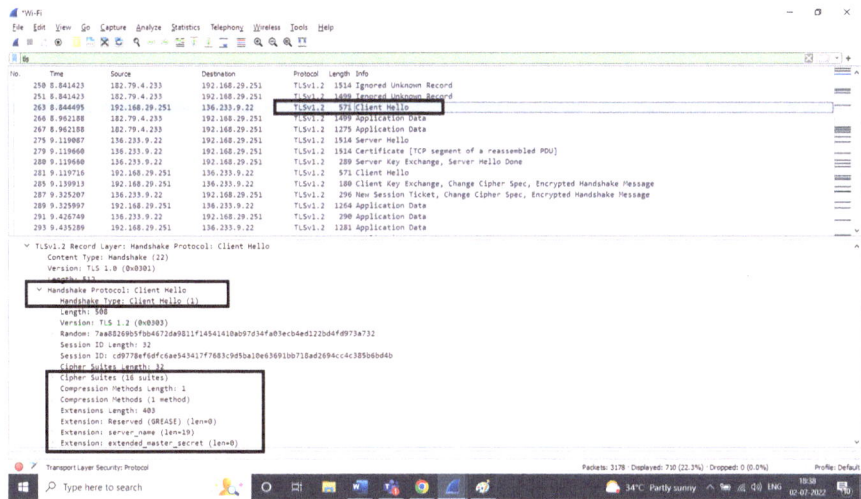

Fig. 1.4   TLS protocol traffic of client hello message

Figure 1.4 shows the illustration of TLS protocol traffic captured while communicating to a web server using HyperText Transfer Protocol Secure (HTTPS) from a local client. A client hello message is the start of the handshake followed by a sequence of messages captured in the top view of the Wireshark panel. The middle view of the tool shows the detailed structure of a client hello TLS packet with various attributes such as TLS version, length of the handshake, session ID, cipher suites length, compression methods and extensions. The extensions contain various information such as server name, master secret key, session ticket, signature algorithms, compress_certificate, supported_versions and padding. Figure 1.5 shows a similar illustration of a server hello message in the Wireshark panel. Most of the attribute fields are similar to the client hello message and the unique attribute is the cipher suite which contains the various encryption and hashing algorithms supported in the server like Elliptic Curve Diffie-Hellman Exchange (ECDHE), Rivest-Shamir-Adleman (RSA) with Advanced Encryption Standard (AES) 256 bit and Secure Hash Algorithm (SHA) 384 bit.

1.4   Security at Application Layer

Application layer in TCP/IP ensures the communications and data exchange between the applications at the both ends of communication. Some of the important protocols such as Pretty Good Privacy (PGP), Secure Multipurpose Internet Mail Extensions (S/MIME), Secure HTTP (HTTPS), Secure Electronic Transactions (SET) ensure the security of the application layer conversations through encryption. An email application uses the S/MIME protocol stack to provide confidentiality,

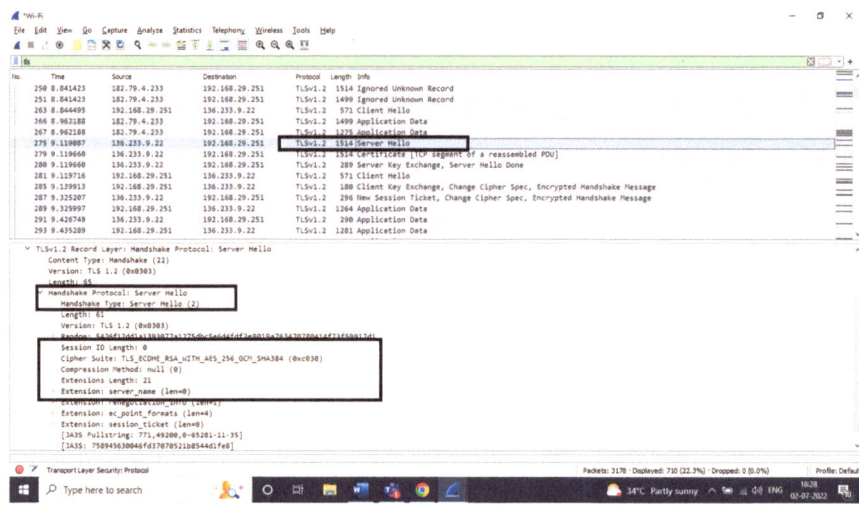

Fig. 1.5 TLS protocol traffic of server hello message

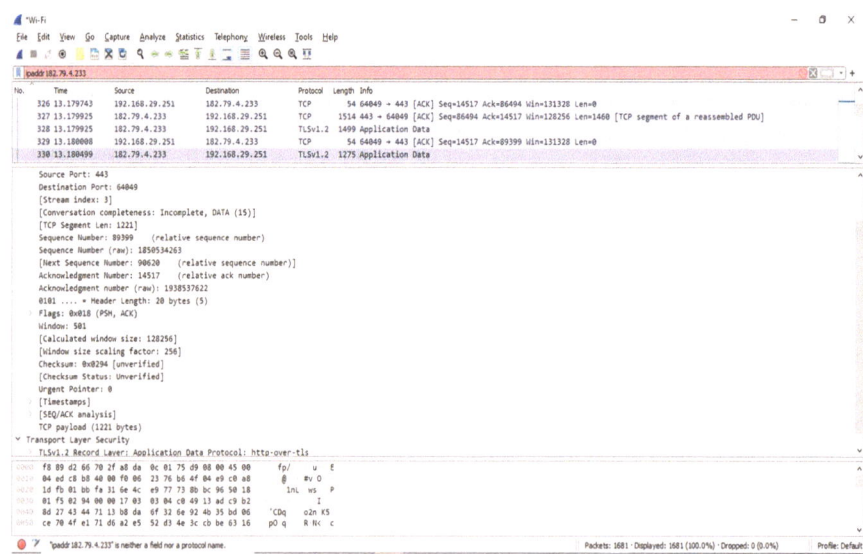

Fig. 1.6 Email traffic

message authentication. S/MIME creates a signature for the message and appends it to the message. Then the message and signature are encrypted using symmetric encryption. The secret key is shared using asymmetric encryption. Figure 1.6 shows a sample email traffic captured in the Wireshark tool while communicating with an email server from a local client. The email server is internally using the TLS protocol for encryption. The sequence of request and response sent and obtained from the email server is shown in the top panel. The middle panel shows the detailed packet structure of an application payload. The various fields which are unencrypted are source port, destination port, sequence number, acknowledgement number, window size and flags. The remaining data is encrypted using TLS 1.2 version protocol. In addition, there are several other application-layer protocols that provide security via encryption to the application data. For example, message stream encryption (MSE) algorithm provides obfuscation, confidentiality and authentication. Some applications such as BitTorrent for file sharing, Voice over IP (VOIP) protocols such as Skype, Zoom and WhatsApp have either their own proprietary encryption protocols or depend on the lower layer protocol suite such as TLS. The other dimension of the security at application layer is to protect from distributed denial-of-service attacks (DDoS), flooding attacks, cross-site scripting, etc. Protection against these threats is ensured with the help of application firewalls. Discussion on this is beyond the scope of this work.

In general, the security protocols in TCP/IP layers follow a phased approach as shown in Fig. 1.7. In this phased approach, the unencrypted communication phases are meant for the initial handshake, cryptographic key exchange and mutual authentication. The encrypted data communication phase provides confidentiality to the

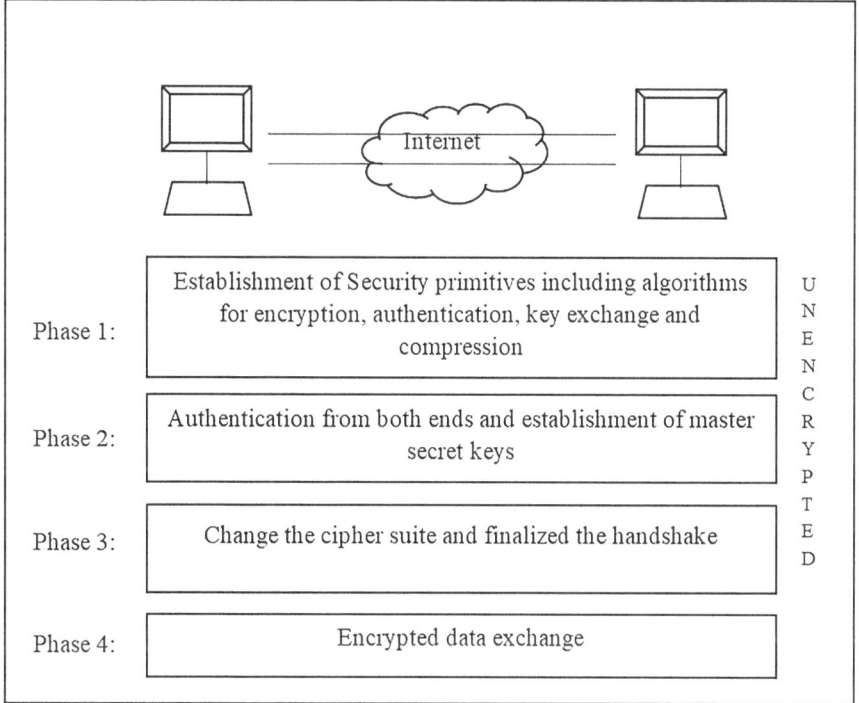

Fig. 1.7 Phased approach of security protocols in TCP/IP

payload. Encryption over network communications is an additional overhead, increasing latency. However, protocols such as TLS are further optimised such that the unencrypted phases between the nodes have become faster. Further, emerging technologies such as quantum computing and 5G/6G networks demand new encryption protocols.

1.5   Security Implementations in Other TCP/IP Networks

The TCP/IP protocol suite is the backbone for processing and routing the data over the Internet. However, the current generation and futuristic use cases, applications requirements of networking and communications have expanded considerably from the scope of TCP/IP. Emerging trends such as software defined networks (SDN), industrial Internet of things (IIoT), video streaming, augmented reality (AR), virtual reality (VR), immersive technology applications, autonomous vehicles, smart applications in agriculture, city and health have different and diversified requirements towards latency, security, quality of service (QoS), etc. Hence there are growing developments towards other networking protocols and standards [3]. Security features to the TCP/IP protocol suite are additional tasks and hence increase communication latency. Table 1.3 shows the security implementation of various other TCP/IP networks.

1.6   Network Traffic Analysis

Network Traffic Analysis (NTA) is an essential task for efficient management and administration of the network. Through this analysis, network administrators manage the performance of the applications, identify deficiencies in the networks, manage unexpected events [4] and have classified various objectives. During the Network Traffic Analysis (NTA), traffic is collected, monitored, stored and analysed. NTA can be based on either the port-based data, packet-based data or flow-based data. There are techniques in the literature that analyse these data items. Port-based techniques analyse the network using the standard port numbers associated with different services and applications. Packet-based techniques inspect the payload content. Hence they are also called payload-based techniques. Flow-based techniques use traffic flow features, the aggregate details captured from the packet headers information. The fundamental assumption made by the flow-based techniques is that the flow features are unique to each application type and can be used by the classifiers. One major challenge in deploying machine learning (ML) is the requirement of labelled data. However, in practical applications, data is available in semi-labelled or unlabelled forms. There are efforts in the literature to deploy deep learning (DL) or active learning techniques to address this problem [5]. The accuracy of any intelligent classifier is based on the features supplied to it as an input. Literature has

Table 1.3 Security implementation in other TCP/IP networks

Other TCP/IP networks	Protocols used	How security is implemented
5G—LTE networks	NAS—Non-access stratum protocol	IPSec
Live audio and video networks and software-defined networks	Flexilink (classification of network packets into flows)	HLS
IOT networks	Zigbee	IPSec or HTTPS
	MQTT	SSL
	AMQP	SSL
	CoAP	DTLS
	XMPP	SSL
	DSS	SSL
Academic institutions networks	RINA—Recursive InterNetwork architecture	HTTPS, SFTP, SSL
IIoT—Industrial internet of things	MQTT—Message queuing telemetry transport, run on TLS/SSL, communication between devices are encrypted and secure AMQP—Advanced message queuing protocol; it allows full suite of messaging patterns CoAP—Constrained application protocol, client-server IoT protocol	SSL SSL DTLS
Vehicular networks	Geo-networking layer coupled with BTP—Basic transport protocol	Cross-layered cognitive security protocol—C2SP
Smart home networks	Zigbee, Z-wave, DNP3—Distributed network protocol, Bluetooth low energy	IPSec or HTTPS
Smart city	Zigbee	IPSec or HTTPS

suggested several features for the analysis. There are ML models are based on the traditional flow features, side-channel features and handshake features that are unencrypted [6]. Though the traffic is encrypted, the above features reveal the details of encrypted traffic.

Monitoring, inspecting and analysing the networked traffic are crucial to securing the network. Further, there are various administration and management benefits in networks. The literature has protocols and tools for collecting and processing network flow records. Table 1.4 summarises some of them. Network flow is a set of related packets that belong to the same transport connection. Some of the flow analysis tools consider flow as unidirectional and some consider it in bidirectional modes. The network flows can be generated either at a network device such as router/firewall or at a host level. Figure 1.8 illustrates different IP flows at the router. This traffic includes application traffic such as email and VoIP traffic, IPSec traffic such as VPN traffic and TLS traffic such as financial transactions.

An IP flow can have the following attributes: IP source address, IP destination address, source port, destination port, layer 3 protocol type, class of service and

Table 1.4 Protocols and standards for traffic flows

S. no	Protocol	Remarks
1	NetFlow	It is developed by Cisco. It records metadata of IP traffic flows to monitor and analyse network flow
2	IPFIX	Internet protocol flow export protocol (IPFIX) is developed by IETF and requests for comments (RFC) 7011. It collects and inspects the flow-related information at network devices
3	J-Flow	It is developed by Juniper networks to monitor, collect and inspect the traffic flow packets from Juniper devices
4	NetStream	It is developed by Huawei to collect and analyse the service traffic based on network flows with a focus on network management
5	sFlow	It is developed by InMon to monitor flow in high speed networks. It supports flow sampling as well
6	Pandora FMS	Flow management system (FMS) developed by Pandora to monitor and analyse the enterprise network resources for efficient management
7	AppFlow	It is a standard for exporting TCP and application layer data. It follows the IPFIX format

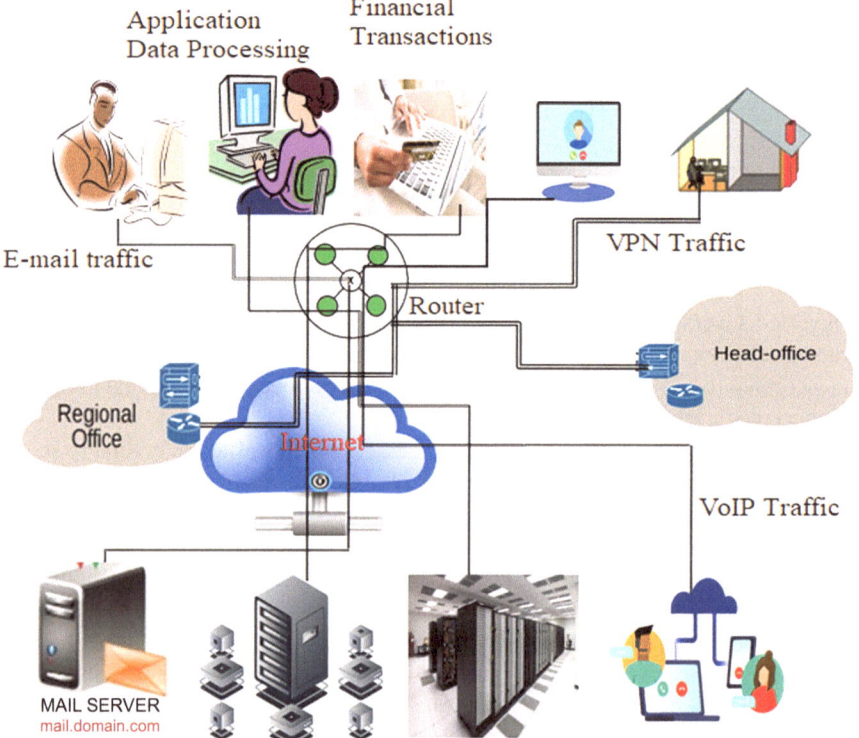

Fig. 1.8 IP flows at router

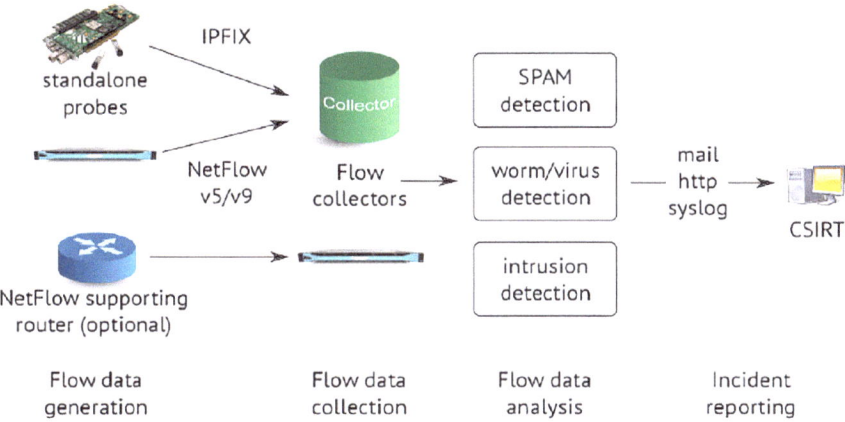

Fig. 1.9 Network monitoring infrastructure [7]

router or switch interface. These flow records mention the volume (size) and type of the traffic but not the content. The network flow collector monitors all the traffic at the network point where it was connected and then generates the network flows. The IETF prepared IPFIX and hence it is regarded as a common standard for IP flows. The IPFIX requires a network monitoring infrastructure as shown in Fig. 1.9 [7].

Cisco has developed the NetFlow protocol to collect, export and analyse massive traffic flow data. NetFlow arranges flow records as NetFlow packets and exports them to the flow collector. Figure 1.10 shows an overview of the NetFlow components. At the router, there may be multiple traffic flows at any given instance of time. Flow record contains the details of flow and statistical details of it. NetFlow V9 is the latest and allows for customisation of flow exports. More details of the same can be obtained from [9].

The flow analysers inspect details from the flow records and analyse traffic by protocol, domain, application, source and destination IPs and ports. This inspection can help detect network resource security or QoS aspects. Flow analyser helps the network admins understand the application, protocol, source and destination details of traffic. But the analyser cannot identify what is exactly inside the flow. However, these flow-based techniques and the tools based on these techniques define the baseline of the traffic. Hence they will classify any network activity other than the baseline as anomaly.

Figure 1.11 shows the flow data captured by NetFlow-enabled device [http://www.cisco.com/en/US/prod/collateral/iosswrel/ps6537/ps6555/ps6601/prod_white_paper0900aecd80406232.html]. NetFlow cache contains thousands, sometimes even millions, of entries capturing the flow details. Once the flow expires, the entries from the cache are exported to the flow collector that further processes the flow particulars to provide the insights about the traffic.

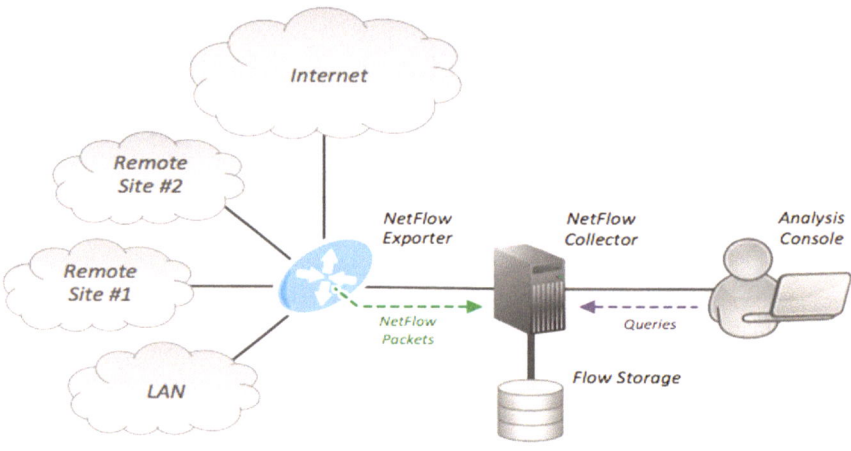

Fig. 1.10 NetFlow overview [8]

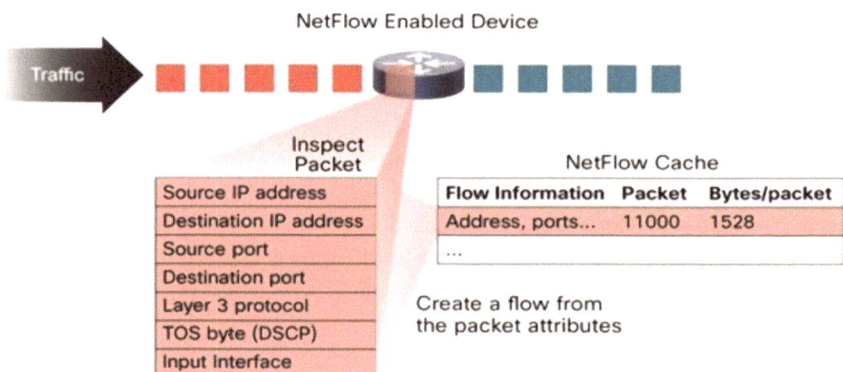

Fig. 1.11 Capturing flow data by NetFlow

1.7 Challenges Involved in Network Traffic Analysis

Analysis of the network traffic is becoming increasingly complex due to the variety of applications and deployment of encryption techniques [10]. The security protocols at different layers of TCP/IP depend on the encryption to protect the in-transit messages from unauthorised access. However, this encrypted traffic is becoming a means to process malicious communication in encapsulated form. So, the malicious threat vectors are leveraging encryption and hence evading the detection of their malicious activities [11]. It is becoming increasingly difficult for enterprises to monitor and inspect encrypted traffic. There are currently solutions that decrypt the traffic and then analyse it [12]. However, it consumes time and network resources. Further, the privacy of the communication gets compromised.

Some of the malware use encrypted communications to command and control servers. Further, enterprise-level data protection and loss-prevention applications cannot monitor, analyse and detect the unauthorised flow of encrypted sensitive data. Further, classical firewall systems, intrusion detection and prevention systems have failed to handle this situation as they depend on analysing the unencrypted traffic. As mentioned above, some of the applications break the encryption, perform the payload inspection, re-encrypt it and forward it to the destination. However, this approach negatively affects the privacy of the communications. Hence there is a huge need for solutions that can analyse the encrypted network traffic without affecting the privacy of the communication. Further, network administrators also need to understand the type of network traffic present in encrypted communications to manage their network resources effectively. Hence inspecting the encrypted network traffic is highly challenging to find a right balance between maintaining the confidentiality of the communication and detecting the potential threats and anomalies within that communication. Researchers and practitioners are trying to implement intelligent techniques to address this problem. Though the traffic is encrypted, certain features of the traffic are still visible for analysis. They include packet header details, statistical properties of traffic flows and temporal details of traffic flows. ML algorithms are deployed to analyse these visible traffic flow features and infer the traffic's information.

Network Traffic Analysis (NTA) has mainly focused on metadata of layer 3 and layer 4 protocols, traffic flow characteristics and flow telemetry. Inspecting the application-layer payload is highly complex and more challenging when encrypted. Some of the enterprises such as Cisco, Juniper networks, etc. have the products that deal with encrypted traffic analytics. These products use network flow characteristics, and behaviour algorithms, to identify the malicious traffic patterns in the encrypted traffic [13–15]. For this purpose, the analysis depends on the metadata of the messages and network flow telemetry. Behaviour-based algorithms learn about what is the normal traffic and then categorise the rest of the traffic as potentially abnormal traffic. These applications include: Cisco Encrypted Traffic Analytics [13]; Cisco IOS Flexible NetFlow [14]; Juniper Advanced Threat Prevention Cloud [15]; ipoque advanced deep packet inspection (DPI) [16]; Arista Network Detection and Response [17]. These solutions use packet, flow, temporal and statistical features and analyse them using machine/deep learning models. Some also combine behavioural and heuristic analysis for fine-grained network traffic analysis. However, learning about what is normal behaviour is a time-consuming task. Further, the systems' dynamic nature makes this a complex task. Traffic patterns that are non-conforming to the regular patterns are often called as anomalies or outliers. Security-related anomalies arise due to inherent vulnerabilities in the design and implementation of the communication and security protocols, hardware, software, etc. [18].

To analyse the encrypted traffic, we need to extract different features and meta data of the encrypted packets, flow of the packets. This includes the unencrypted details from the initial handshakes, encrypted payload and statistical properties of packets flow. Data can be collected either at the client or at the network level.

Client-level data can be captured using event logs, inbound and outbound traffic collected at the IP level. At the network-level packet traces, flow-level data can be collected using the probes located at network links. For example, the traces can be the HTTPS communication between client and web server using TLS. Generally, IP traffic flows are preferred for the analysis than the packet traces. Though packet-level data describes the traffic in a detailed manner, analysing those details is computationally intensive. Alternatively, IP packets are aggregated as IP packet flows for analysis purposes [19]. But for that, the flow feature set and flow exporters must be defined. However, this definition of features is based on specific research objectives and goals. As per the RFC 5470 definition of basic IP flows, flow information provides details such as who was involved in the communication, temporal details and the amount of data transferred. However, there are several extensions that can be used to extract more details about IP flows [20]. Some techniques in the literature perform sampling of the traffic flows [21].

Classification of the network traffic is an essential task in network traffic analysis and it is required for multiple reasons. ML-based techniques such as Naïve Bayes, decision trees, support vector machine (svm), etc. are used for network traffic classification [22, 23]. They are used to classify the traffic such as HTTP, Domain Name System (DNS) and simple mail transfer protocol (SMTP). The primary challenge in processing and analysing the encrypted traffic is extracting the traffic's relevant features. Models can use the statistical features related to the packets and flow data available from the unencrypted fields during the handshake process shown in Fig. 1.7. Deep learning models can help to build the features automatically [24, 25]. Next chapter provides a detailed analysis on the methodology of encrypted network traffic analysis, collecting the network traffic data for analysis and preprocessing, different publicly available datasets from multiple sources, feature selection and processing, techniques and performance measures for encrypted traffic analysis.

1.8 Conclusions

This chapter has provided the foundations of encrypted traffic analysis. We have discussed the security in TCP/IP protocol stack, how the network traffic is encrypted at different layers, the need for traffic analysis and challenges involved in analysing the encrypted network traffic. Further we have also discussed the packet-based and flow-based analysis approaches for network traffic analysis.

References

1. Stallings, W. (2022). *Cryptography and network security, 8/E*. Pearson Education India.
2. Forouzan, B. A. (2017). *TCP/IP protocol suite*. McGraw-Hill Higher Education.

3. Goralski, W. (2017). *The illustrated network: How TCP/IP works in a modern network.* Morgan Kaufmann.

4. Boutaba, R., Salahuddin, M. A., Limam, N., Ayoubi, S., Shahriar, N., Estrada-Solano, F., & Caicedo, O. M. (2018). A comprehensive survey on machine learning for networking: Evolution, applications and research opportunities. *Journal of Internet Services and Applications, 9*(1), 1–99.

5. Shahraki, A., Abbasi, M., Taherkordi, A., & Jurcut, A. D. (2021). Active learning for network traffic classification: A technical study. *IEEE Transactions on Cognitive Communications and Networking, 8*(1), 422–439.

6. Anderson, B., Paul, S., & McGrew, D. (2018). Deciphering malware's use of TLS (without decryption). *Journal of Computer Virology and Hacking Techniques, 14*, 195–211.

7. Nemec, B. A. (2016). *Security course: Network traffic monitoring.* https://is.muni.cz/th/yqkg2/dp.pdf

8. https://en.wikipedia.org/wiki/NetFlow

9. https://www.cisco.com/en/US/technologies/tk648/tk362/technologies_white_paper09186a00800a3db9.html

10. European Union Agency for Cybersecurity (ENISA) Report. (2020). *Encrypted traffic analysis: Use cases security challenges.*

11. Lueck, M. (2021). The seven myths of encrypted traffic scanning. *Network Security, 2021*(7), 9–12.

12. Velan, P., Čermák, M., Čeleda, P., & Drašar, M. (2015). A survey of methods for encrypted traffic classification and analysis. *International Journal of Network Management, 25*(5), 355–374.

13. https://www.cisco.com/c/en/us/solutions/collateral/enterprise-networks/enterprise-network-security/nb-09-encrytd-traf-anlytcs-wp-cte-en.html

14. https://www.cisco.com/c/en/us/td/docs/ios-xml/ios/fnetflow/configuration/xe-16-12/fnf-xe-17-book/fnf-fnetflow.pdf

15. https://www.juniper.net/documentation/product/us/en/juniper-sky-advanced-threat-prevention

16. https://www.ipoque.com/

17. https://www.arista.com/en/products/network-detection-and-response

18. Bhattacharyya, D. K., & Kalita, J. K. (2013). *Network anomaly detection: A machine learning perspective.* CRC Press.

19. Anderson, B., & McGrew, D. (2016). Identifying encrypted malware traffic with contextual flow data. In *Proceedings of the 2016 ACM workshop on artificial intelligence and security* (pp. 354–356).

20. https://www.rfc-editor.org/rfc/rfc5470

21. Niu, W., Zhuo, Z., Zhang, X., Du, X., Yang, G., & Guizani, M. (2019). A heuristic statistical testing based approach for encrypted network traffic identification. *IEEE Transactions on Vehicular Technology, 68*(4), 3843–3853.

22. Shen, M., Ye, K., Liu, X., Zhu, L., Kang, J., Yu, S., Li, Q., & Xu, K. (2022). Machine learning-powered encrypted network traffic analysis: A comprehensive survey. *IEEE Communications Surveys & Tutorials.*

23. Kohout, J., Komárek, T., Čech, P., Bodnár, J., & Lokoč, J. (2018). Learning communication patterns for malware discovery in HTTPs data. *Expert Systems with Applications, 101*, 129–142.

24. Abbasi, M., Shahraki, A., & Taherkordi, A. (2021). Deep learning for network traffic monitoring and analysis (NTMA): A survey. *Computer Communications, 170*, 19–41.

25. Islam, F. U., Liu, G., Liu, W., & Haq, Q. M. U. (2023). A deep learning-based framework to identify and characterise heterogeneous secure network traffic. *IET Information Security, 17*(2), 294–308.

Chapter 2
Encrypted Network Traffic Analysis

2.1 Introduction

As per the Google report [1], 99% of the Internet traffic is encrypted to provide privacy and security to the data during the transmission. However, under the guise of encryption, malicious actors pose several threats. Encrypted Network Traffic Analysis (ENTA) is the process of analysing Internet traffic that is encrypted using different encryption protocols, to gain various insights about the nature of the traffic. ENTA can be used by the network administrators and security professionals to safeguard the uses of data, communications, network infrastructure, etc. The conventional application firewalls, intrusion detection systems (IDS), etc. analyse only unencrypted traffic and hence cannot handle ENTA. Techniques such as deep packet inspection (DPI) try to break the encryption to analyse the traffic, though they violate privacy of the users and bring several other security issues. Techniques such as port-based traffic classification are of no use for encrypted traffic analysis. Current research in this area is using machine learning (ML) models to identify and classify encrypted malicious traffic without decrypting it. Through statistical and intelligent techniques, ENTA can detect suspicious encrypted traffic, identify encrypted communications between malware command and control servers and targeted systems.

Statistical, ML-based models analyse various features including packets, flows, sessions, connections, etc. of the encrypted traffic and learn patterns in the traffic. This learning helps the models to derive the inferences about the encrypted network traffic. By analysing the properties of encrypted data, it is possible to create application fingerprinting so as to understand the encrypted requests of the users. Similarly by analysing the features of traffic flows, using ML models, encrypted protocols traffic can be classified and identified with a reasonably better accuracy. Information theoretic techniques, statistical techniques, ML/DL-based techniques do not depend on the deep packet analysis. These techniques leverage on the features that are less prone to encryption protocols. Further, DL-based techniques handle the issues related to feature extraction.

ENTA can be used for both legitimate and illegitimate purposes. While ENTA has potential benefits in providing security, it also poses several challenges and threats. ENTA can even be performed by the malicious actors. Through analysis, attackers can understand the applications on the device; the websites that users visit, even in anonymous networks such as ToR; identify user actions and download. So ENTA provides a lot of information about users and their actions. It is highly challenging to detect malicious communications in encrypted traffic than in unencrypted traffic. As encryption conceals the payload data, it has substantial influence on the network management and on the security infrastructure such as firewalls and intrusion detection systems. Malicious actors exploit this for their operations. While this can be mitigated by inspecting and examining the TLS traffic certificates and payload descriptions, it violates the privacy of the sensitive and important communications. Hence managing the right balance between the privacy of the communications, end-to-end security and analysing the encrypted traffic for security reasons is essential.

2.2   ENTA Methodology

Most of the literature on network traffic analysis focuses on network performance [2]. However in the recent past, there is a growing literature on ENTA for security issues. There are few broad frameworks in the literature, providing guidelines on the way an ENTA can be performed. Velan et al. [3] have categorised the ENTA based on the three parameters, namely input that is considered for the analysis including payload, traffic properties and output of the analysis. Zhao et al. [4] have provided a broad methodology for network traffic classification. Their proposal focuses on collecting the data items to create dataset, feature selection, decision-making for classification and evaluation. However, their focus was not on encrypted traffic. Papadogiannaki and Ioannidis [5] have provided a top-down view of ENTA, i.e. from use cases to the objectives of analysis. Further, their focus was also about countermeasures towards using ENTA for adversarial activities such as breaching privacy and confidentiality. Wang et al. [6] have provided a general framework of machine learning-based encrypted traffic detection. Their framework is a more generic approach that would fit into any encrypted traffic analysis problem. Recently, Shen et al. [7] also have provided taxonomy of ENTA according to the goals of the analysis. They provided a general workflow of ML-based ENTA. Feng et al. [8] have provided a general data-processing pipeline for fine-grained traffic analysis. A technical report from European Union Agency for Cybersecurity (ENISA) has also discussed taxonomy of ENTA, purpose of the analysis, information extraction methodology (for feature generation and selection) and information processing methodology [9]. From the study of these resources, we categorise ENTA based on the following parameters: goal, purpose and objective of performing ENTA; traffic-related information used for analysis, i.e. features used for the analysis including feature extraction and selection; techniques applied over the traffic information.

These broad categories can further be analysed in a fine-grained manner as different steps in ENTA. Figure 2.1 provides a broad summary of the different steps involved in the ENTA. The first step in performing the ENTA is to identify the purpose of the analysis. Based on the purpose and objective of the analysis, further course of action can be designed. The outcome of ENTA is to ensure quality of service, security, activity and behaviour modelling. Hence research objectives can be classifying encrypted traffic, detecting the malicious traffic in the encrypted communication, optimising the network resources and quality of service, etc. Figure 2.1 lists different objectives in each step. Once the objectives are fixed, then the next step would be to collect the relevant data. There are few phases involved in data collection, starting from identifying the location of data collection. There are several tools to collect the data and there are publicly available datasets as well. Collected data should be preprocessed to handle several issues in the data. Section 2.3 provides a detailed description of data collection and preprocessing. Feature selection and relevant feature extraction are important phases in ENTA. Features can either be available in the data intrinsically or alternatively features can be derived statistically. Section 2.4 has provided a detailed analysis on the feature selection and extraction. Selected features help the techniques to perform required analysis. There are several techniques such as deep packet inspection, statistical analysis, machine learning and deep learning-based techniques to analyse the features. Performance of the techniques can be analysed through different metrics. Section 2.6 discusses various metrics to measure the performance of ENTA.

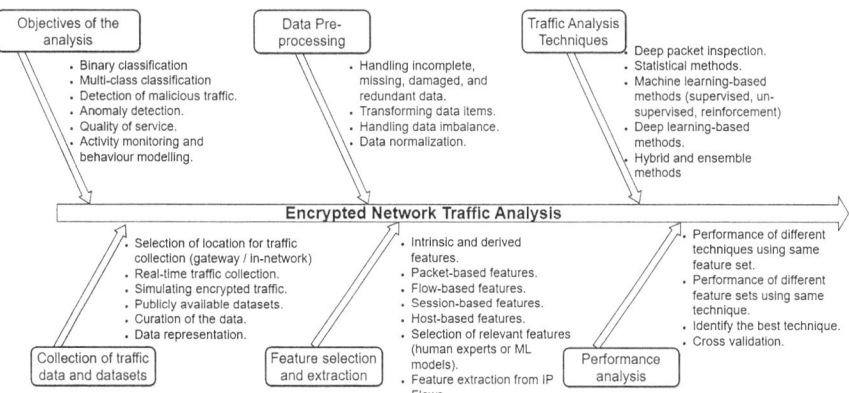

Fig. 2.1 Steps involved in ENTA

2.3 Purpose of the Analysis

Objective of the ENTA can be broadly classified as classification and detection/ identification. There are several tasks and analyses that can be performed from these objectives. Table 2.1 provides a more detailed summary of ENTA based on the research objectives. ENTA can be regarded as multi-objective and multi-tasked analysis. Traffic classification can further be subdivided into various tasks that are either binary classification or multiclass classification problems. While performing either of these classifications, the analysis can either be focusing on specific set of protocols such as DNS, Quick UDP Internet Connections (QUIC), VPN and P2P (peer-to-peer) or it can be protocol agnostic. Encrypted malicious traffic classification is a multiclass classification task in classifying the traffic based on multiple or different malware families. Further, this analysis also can be protocol-specific or agnostic. There are several works in the literature in addressing these objectives in varieties of traffic environments [3, 5, 6, 8]. Traffic detection and identification aim

Table 2.1 Objectives and tasks of ENTA

Objective: traffic classification	
S. no	Analysis task
1.	Binary classification of network traffic as unencrypted and encrypted traffic without any specific protocol
2.	Binary classification of traffic for specific set of protocols
3.	Binary classification of encrypted traffic into malicious and non-malicious without any specific set of protocols
4.	Binary classification of encrypted traffic into malicious and non-malicious under specific set of protocols
5.	Multiclass classification of malicious encrypted traffic without any specific set of protocols
6.	Multiclass classification of malicious encrypted traffic with a specific set of protocols
Objective: traffic identification and detection	
S. no	Analysis task
1	Identification of particular application or protocol-specific traffic in encrypted communication
2	Anomaly detection or suspicious traffic pattern detection in encrypted communications
3.	Identification of malicious communications between command & control servers and targeted machines
4.	Identification of user information and activity monitoring
5.	Identification and creation of user or device fingerprinting
6.	Detecting privacy leakages in encrypted communications
7.	Inspect the encrypted traffic to characterise and measure the quality of service and optimisation
8.	Detection of unknown encrypted malicious traffic

at detecting specific application or protocol-based traffic in encrypted communication. The most challenging aspect is the detection of unknown traffic.

Once the objective and tasks are finalised, then accordingly, network traffic collection, feature selection and extraction, model building and evaluation follow in the order. The analysis has significance in ensuring the security of the networked communications and also mitigating the challenges from the malicious actors.

The available literature on ENTA deals with either one or multiple objectives and tasks that are listed in Table 2.1. One of the important parameters that needs to be considered during the task implementation is the location of deployment of the model for detection, i.e. whether the analysis to be conducted offline or online. Based on the research objectives and the tasks identified, relevant data has to be collected and a dataset be created to train the model. Next section deals with the collection of traffic data using which a model can be trained.

2.4   Collection of Traffic Data and Preprocessing

According to the research task(s), appropriate data has to be collected for the analysis. For training, the data can be collected real time or be simulated. For real-time analysis, the traffic generated by different devices is collected by the gateways, firewalls, ISP's and servers through traffic monitors. This traffic is analysed by the systems that are trained by different statistical or machine learning or data analysis engines. There are various network traffic monitoring and analysis tools [10]. Table 2.2 provides various tools that are available for the collection and analysis of encrypted traffic. Some are open source and a few are commercial. Also they work at different layers of TCP/IP protocol stack. One of the major challenges with the real-time traffic data collection and using the same for training the model is the data imbalance problem. Obtaining sufficient malicious traffic to train the model is highly challenging. Alternatively, there are network traffic simulators that can simulate the network traffic as per the requirement. Table 2.3 provides some of the network simulators that create network traffic.

The dataset whether it is created real-time or simulated should have following characteristics such as large and sufficient amount of training data; represent variety of protocols, applications, attack types, etc. based on the objectives; rightly balanced; well confirmed ground truth data.

These characteristics of the data are essential to build robust and highly accurate ENTA models. There are several publicly available datasets specific to particular type of application, protocol and attack. Table 2.4 summarises several widely available datasets. These datasets are diverse in nature in terms of traffic types, attack types, availability of encrypted traffic, availability of malicious samples, etc. Canadian Institute for Cybersecurity (CIC) has curated several datasets that can be used for experiments (https://www.unb.ca/cic/datasets/index.html).

Finding datasets that are relevant and suitable to the objectives of the work is highly challenging due to the sensitive nature of the traffic. Some of the works

Table 2.2 Tools for real-time traffic data collection

S. no	Tool	Description
1	Tcpdump [11]	Command-line application to collect, inspect and analyse the network traffic. It can be used for non-TCP traffic as well
2	WireShark [12]	Multi-purpose, open source packet capture and analyser tool that can capture packets in real time. It can analyse the packets captured by other applications in offline
3.	Smartsniff [13]	Network monitoring tool that allows to collect TCP/IP packets
4	Cloudshark [14]	Network analysis solution that captures packets and organise, share and analyse them.
5	Ngrep [15]	Linux-based network packet analyser that works at network layer by matching regular expressions of payloads
6	NetMate [16]	It is a simple network measurement and accounting system that can generate network traffic flows from raw packets
7	Libcap [11]	An open source API to build applications for capturing the packets
8	Snort [17]	Rule-based engine to sniff, log and analyse the traffic packets
9	Omnipeek [18]	Packet capture, deep packet analysis and visualisation tool that work with different protocols and data types
10	Zeek [19]	Open source and passive tool that help to analyse the network traffic packets
11	Ettercap [20]	Tool to sniff the live packets and analyse the traffic with a focus on man-in-middle attacks
13	Suricata [21]	Open source tool to analyse the network traffic with a focus on intrusion detection and prevention
14.	WinPcap [22]	Tool for capturing, filtering and transmitting network packets

reported in the literature have used even their own proprietary datasets. Datasets having malicious traffic samples are either few or the number of samples in the datasets is limited. To address the challenge of data availability and to facilitate research in this domain, Wang et al. [6] have composed a dataset from the commonly available, multiple, public datasets. Their dataset satisfies the criteria such as right mixture of malicious and non-malicious traffic, traffic from multiple devices including conventional and IoT devices and equal distribution of traffic size from each of the public datasets. There are several traffic collection engines that collect data as per the requirement [8].

Figure 2.2 shows a comprehensive overview of dataset types, different data items, features that can be extracted from the datasets. Generally, the traffic data is stored in the form of Packet Capture (PCAP) or Packet Capture Next Generation (PCAPNG). A data preprocessing step has to be conducted on this data to remove irrelevant details, incomplete, duplicate, damaged packet details that are not useful to the analysis. Some of the protocols such as Address resolution protocol (ARP) and Internet control message protocol (ICMP) do not contribute to ENTA. So,

Table 2.3 Tools for network traffic data simulation

S. no	Tool	Description
1	NS3 [23]	Tool to simulate real-world networks. Also it generates the PCAP files which can further be analysed using tools such as Wireshark
2	Packet Tracer [24]	Simulation tool from Cisco to create virtually different network topologies and capture the packets
3	NPing [25]	Open source tool to generate network packets across wide range of protocols
4	Ostinato [26]	Tool to generate PCAP files and network traffic of different kinds
5	Netscan tools pro [27]	It is an integrated set of utilities including packet generation, flooder and capturing
6	WANkiller [28]	Traffic generator tool with a focus on real-time network monitoring and stress testing
7	Netropy [29]	Helps to create background traffic using PCAP files
8	Bit-twist packet generator [30]	Open source Ethernet packet generator and editor tool
9	TCPReplay [22]	Open source utilities that help in editing and replaying already captured network traffic

details about such protocols can be avoided from the data. Further, data preprocessing should also convert categorical data to the numerical data. If the data is imbalanced, then techniques such as data augmentation, oversampling or undersampling and Synthetic Minority Over-Sampling Technique (SMOTE) are used. Data normalisation is another important preprocessing step to make the data ready for further analysis.

Typically the network traffic data is collected at the gateway of the network. Hence the bidirectional traffic, i.e. inbound and outbound, would be collected for analysis. In addition, traffic can be collected in the middle of network as well. If Internet service provider (ISP) or Internet exchange point (IXP) is doing the traffic analysis, then the large amount of traffic can be captured. However, there are concerns that such data would typically be in one direction. Hence a gateway-based traffic collection is preferred for fine-gained traffic analysis [8].

Traffic data can be broadly classified into packet level and flow level. Packet-level data contain raw network traffic details, packet header and payload details. However, the task is highly complex and increases communication and computation overload significantly. Hence flow-based analysis is preferred than packet-based analysis. Flow is either a 5-tuple or a 3-tuple representation which contains source IP, destination IP, source TCP port, destination TCP port and IP protocol. A 3-tuple flow can have source and destination IP address and IP protocol details. Flow-level data collection engines aggregate relevant packets into a flow and then extracts metadata or statistical details of the flow. Traffic flow-based analysis can overcome the computational and communication overloads that packet-based analysis suffer. There are industry-based methods such as sFlow defined in RFC 3176 that copy first N bytes of packet. One commonly used flow-level data capture engine is NetFlow Analyzer [61], which captures the flow information details of each direction

Table 2.4 Datasets (unencrypted and encrypted) available for ENTA

S. no	Dataset	Description
1	MTA [31]	Contains different types of malware-infected traffic including ransomware. PCAP files are indicated as malicious
2	USTC-TFC2016 [32]	Unencrypted normal and malicious traffic. The dataset has two parts. First part contains 10 different classes of malware traffic such as Htbot, Neris, Tinba, etc. second part contains 10 different types of normal traffic such as BiTorrent, P2P, email, video, etc.
3	ISCXVPN2016 [33]	Labelled network traffic (VPN and non-VPN). The dataset has 14 different categories of traffic dealing with VOIP, VPN-VOIP, P2P, VPN-P2P, etc. different types of traffic include browsing, email, hat, streaming, VoIP and TraP2P
4	ISCXTor2016 [33]	Labelled tor and non-tor network traffic dataset. Tor traffic contains seven different categories of traffic. This includes email, chats, P2P, VoIP, audio and video streaming data
5	ISCX-URL 2016 [34]	Labelled dataset with over 1,10,000 URLs. Benign, spam, phishing, malware, defacement URLs
6	ISCX Android Botnet 2015 [35]	Android botnet dataset with labels. Android botnet 14 different families and 1929 samples
7	ISCX Botnet 2014 [36]	Dataset with overlapping subsets of multiple datasets. The dataset combines ISOT, ISCX 2012 IDS, malware capture facility project datasets having normal and malicious traffic flows
8	CIC-Darknet 2020 [37]	Encrypted traffic and non-encrypted flows of Darknet traffic. Dataset is related to different types of Darknet traffic including audio and video streams, chat, email and VOIP
11	CIC Bell DNS EXF 2021 [38],	Labelled dataset for DNS data exfiltration attack traffic. Dataset with two categories of light file attack and heavy file attack with multiple types of files
12	CIC Bell DNS 2021 [39]	Large DNS features dataset based on malicious and benign domains. Dataset with different features from more than one million domains categorised as benign, spam, phishing, malware
13	CIC-DDoS 2019 [40]	Labelled dataset with benign and common DDoS attacks. Also labelled flow data. Raw data is in PCAP mode. Also it has 80 features extracted with the help of CICFlowMeter
14	CIC-IDS 2017 [41], CSE-CIC-IDS 2018 [41]	Labelled datasets about IDS. CIC-IDS 2017 contains benign and most common IDS attacks resembling PCAP mode. It also include labelled flows of the traffic. CIC-IDS 2018 contain seven different attack scenarios and 80 extracted features
15	CIC IoT 2023 [42]	Labelled dataset with IoT network benign and malicious traffic. IoT attack dataset with 33 different attacks categorised into seven types
16	CIRA-CIC-DoHBrw-2020 [43]	DoH and Non-DoH traffic. The dataset has malicious and benign DoH and Non-DoH traffic. The dataset is created with a layered approach where in the first layer traffic is classified as DoH and non-DoH traffic with the help of statistical features. In the second layer, DoH traffic is classified as benign and malicious
17	VIT_SPARC20 [44]	Labelled unencrypted and encrypted normal and malicious traffic. Contains HTTP and HTTPS traffic of various applications

(continued)

Table 2.4 (continued)

S. no	Dataset	Description
20	NSL KDD [45]	Labelled IDS dataset with records of Internet traffic. Modified version of KDD 99 data. Traffic records with 43 features per each record and with binary labels of benign and attack. Further, attacks are categorised into four different types such as DoS, Probe, U2R, R2L and each type has different sub-classes of attacks
23	ISCX-IDS-2012 [46]	Labelled dataset with full packet payloads in PCAP format. Dataset meant for evaluating intrusion detection models with diverse intrusion scenarios. It contains both normal and malicious activity packets
24	ADFA-LD and ADFA-WD [47]	Labelled dataset containing call traces for exploits and attacks. Linux and Windows-based datasets for evaluating host-based intrusion detection
25	InSDN [48]	Labelled realistic traffic with both packet and flow traffic environment is software-defined networks Anomaly detection dataset for SDN networks. Attack traffic including botnet, DoS, DDoS, etc.
26.	Kyoto dataset [49]	Real network traffic with several statistical features and attack types. Traces from mail and DNS with normal and malicious traffic
27.	MAWI traces [50]	Labelled dataset for anomaly detection. Traffic anomalies with labels such as anomalous, suspicious, notice and benign
29.	IMTD17 [51]	Labelled and unlabelled traffic with mobile application traffic flows
30.	Moore [52]	Different categories of two-way network traffic flows
31	Mirage-2019 [43]	Mobile traffic analysis dataset that contains traffic generated by 40 mobile applications in multiple devices
32	IoT encrypted traffic data [53]	IoT traffic from multiple IoT devices collected under different settings including single device, multiple devices and VPN. The dataset also has non-IoT traffic
33	UNSW_NS 2015 [54]	Labelled dataset deals exclusively with nine different intrusion detection attacks. The dataset has 49 features dealing with traffic. The dataset is created using IXIA traffic generator tool
34	UNSW_NS 2019 [55]	Contains two datasets including raw packet traces and derived flows captured from different IoT devices. Further, the dataset has legitimate and malicious encrypted traffic
35	MIRAGE-2019 [56]	Mobile application traffic from 40 different mobile applications including e-commerce, social network, video and audio. The dataset contains details such as per packet data, per flow features and per-flow metadata
36	CIC-AndMal 2017 [57]	The dataset deals with Android benign and with 42 malware traffic samples and more than 80 features of traffic flow
37	FIRST 2015 [58]	PCAP files and encrypted traffic with different attack types
38	CTU-13 [59]	Labelled dataset with normal, botnet and background traffic. It has 13 scenarios of different botnet samples. PCAPs are processed to obtain flows and logs
39	Malware capture facility project [59]	Dataset contains background traffic and malware dataset
40	WebIdent traces [60]	Encrypted SSH tunnel traffic dataset with a limited set of traffic features

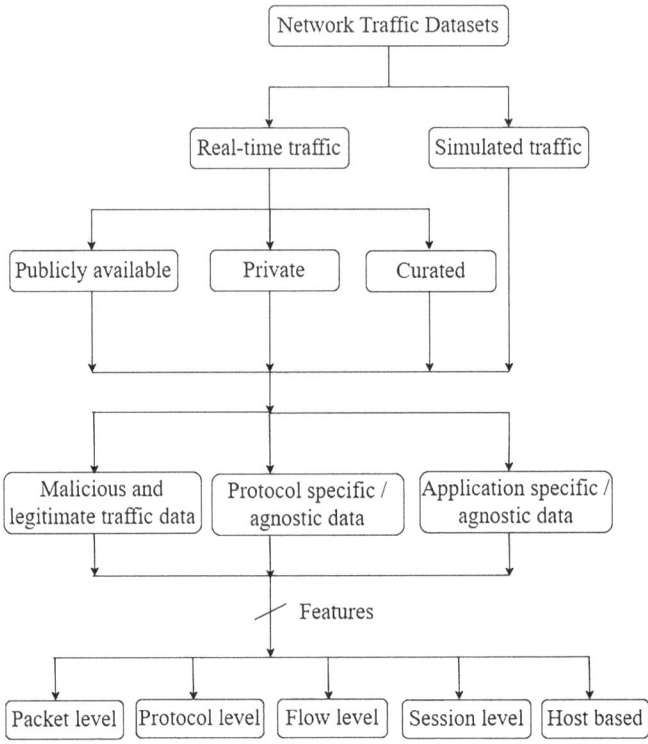

Fig. 2.2 Dataset types, data items, features

independently. This allows a fine-grained analysis of traffic. The other flow capture mechanisms include Argus, Cflowd, J-Flow, NetStream, remote network monitoring (RMON). While collecting traffic data, another major challenge is the velocity of the traffic. There are other frameworks such as Netmap, eXpress Data Path (XDP), hXDP, Netseer that can handle the challenge. Datasets can be categorised based on the type of traffic such as mobile traffic, TLS/SSL traffic, IoT traffic, DNS traffic and VPN traffic: encrypted or unencrypted, malicious or non-malicious communications. However, building the classification or detection models would be challenging if the datasets are not labelled and details about encrypted traffic and original PCAP files are not available.

2.5   Feature Selection and Extraction

The next step of ENTA is to extract the features that are relevant for the analysis from network traffic datasets. The challenging aspect of this extraction is to identify the relevant features and understand their characteristics. Available literature has classified the features into multiple categories. Velan et al. [3] have classified the measurable traffic features into packet-based, flow-based, host-based and host community-based features. Zhao et al. [4] have categorised the traffic features into four levels as packet level, flow level, connection level and host level. Shen et al. [7] have identified the categories broadly as packet based, statistical features and raw traffic representations in which features are extracted by the deep learning algorithms. Feng et al. [8] have broadly categorised the features as intrinsic features and derived features. Intrinsic features are directly obtained from the network traffic data. They are further classified as packet-based and flow-based intrinsic features. Packet size, packet interval, first N bytes of payload, etc. are the examples for packet-based intrinsic features. Similarly flow size, flow duration, etc. are the intrinsic flow-based features. Derived features cannot be directly extracted from the raw traffic data. Instead, they should be extracted using a statistical or data analytic techniques. Derived features are further subdivided into packet based, flow based and session based. Generally derived features provide more fine-grained information about the network traffic. However, generating the derived features is complex and expensive.

Wang et al. [6] have provided a more detailed classification of traffic features. Initially they have categorised features into protocol agnostic and protocol-specific features. There are around 113 protocol agnostic numerical features. They show various statistical details of the traffic. Typically, they are the derived features that are calculated from the network traffic. Protocol agnostic features are further classified into packet based, session based and flow based. In addition, statistical or data analytics-based feature engineering can be applied on these features. There are works in the literature that perform ENTA using these features. Liu et al. [62] have provided subcategories to these features as TCP/IP header features, temporal features, length related features and packet variation features. Protocol-specific features provide details about the encrypted protocols such as TLS/SSL and digital certificates X.509. However, the major limitation is that the protocol-specific features are applicable only to the corresponding protocol and hence will not be useful to analyse other protocol traffic. Protocol-specific features are generally extracted from the log files.

Bazuhair and Lee [63] have analysed the malware-based encrypted communications. For this purpose, they have categorised the features into connection features, SSL features and certificate features. Examples of connection features are number of SSL aggregators and connection records, mean of duration, standard deviation of duration, inbound packets number and outbound packet number. SSL features are ratio of connection records and SSL aggregations, ratio of TLS and SSL versions, etc. Every TLS connection between client and server requires exchange of certificates. Hence certificate log files contain details of the certificates. Examples for the certificate features are average key length, average certificate length, number of different certificates, number of domains in the certificates, number of signed certificates path, public key mean, mean of certificate, validity of periods and validity of certificate period [63–65].

2.5.1 Packet-Based Features

Jing et al. [66] have provided a detailed analysis on how different data items such as packet level, flow level, connection level and host level can be analysed for security threat detection. Packet-based features are generally easy to obtain. The basic 5-tuple packet-based feature, i.e. source and destination addresses, source and destination ports, protocol information, is an intrinsic feature set. In addition, we can also derive features such as inter-arrival time of packet and statistical values of the packets. Table 2.5 provides summary of important packet-level features. Packet size is different between unencrypted and encrypted traffic. Hence it helps in classifying the traffic. Similarly, encrypted traffic will have consistent packet timing than the unencrypted traffic. Packet entropy values are higher for encrypted traffic than unencrypted traffic. Packet length distribution of encrypted traffic is different from that of unencrypted traffic. While packet payload of encrypted traffic does not reveal much details, its metadata would provide more insights. Packet-level features are extracted from the network traffic packets that pass through various network-level interfaces. Subsequently, these features are exported and analysed. Hence collecting and analysing packet-level features are expensive and not scalable.

2.5.1.1 Flow-Based Features

A flow can be described as the collection of packets that share the same 5-tuple data and observed in a given interval of time. Flow-based features provide aggregated details of the network traffic. Hence the amount of data to be analysed decreases drastically when compared with packet-based features. Flow-level features describe the properties of flow of the network traffic. They provide high-level insights on the

Table 2.5 Packet-based features

S. no	Feature	Description
1.	Packet size	Length of a network traffic packet given in bytes
2.	Packet source address	Source IP address of the packet
3.	Packet destination address	Destination IP address of the packet
4.	Source port	Port number of the packet source
5.	Destination port	Port number of the packet destination
6.	Protocol	Application protocol governing the packet
7.	Inter-arrival time	The time of packet arrival
8.	Number of packets	Total number of packets transferred during a given amount of time
9.	Packet-based statistical features such as mean, median, max, min, variance and standard deviation	These are the various statistical features that can be derived for packet size and also packet inter-arrival time

network traffic through addresses, ports, bytes and packet counts. Moore et al. [52] have provided a set of 250 flow-based features. They defined flow as a set of first few packets travelling between source and destination using a protocol. Flow can be unidirectional or bidirectional. They have categorised flow as idle flow, where there are no packets between hosts for more than 2 s; interactive flow in which packets travel in both directions and bulk flow in which packets flow only unidirectional and only acknowledgement from the other node.

While the basic flow-level features are intrinsic, there are several features that can be derived. Table 2.6 provides flow-level features that are used for ENTA. As we can observe from the table, flow-based features capture the different characteristics of the flows. They are mostly derived features of the traffic. Literature has widely reported various works that consider flow-based features. Flow duration, size distribution and direction can provide the details on the type of communication. Similarly, flow rate provides insights on the bandwidth requirements of encrypted communication.

Flow level-based mechanisms work on the basic assumption that benign and malicious communications differ with significant statistical characteristics. Hence they identify the network sources with corresponding attack/benign categories. This identification uses the IP flow characteristics and statistics such as inter-arrival time, flow duration and average packet analysis. Based on these characteristics, literature has identified the traffic discriminators. Further there are techniques that examine the flows for shorter time intervals to understand the changes in the flow [67, 68]. Very recently Chen et al. [69] have proposed encrypted traffic classification method that analyses multiple flows, instead of a single flow. Their method formed a flow bunch called bag of flows, from multiple flow triples, i.e. destination IP, destination port and protocol. This flow bunch is created by clustering similar multiple flows based on the statistical features of the flows. These features categorised as general protocol-related features, time-dependent features, quantity-related features and length-dependent features. Flow bunches are further analysed of multi-flow application classification. For this purpose different classification schemas are proposed [69]. However, there are inherent challenges with flow-based features. While flow-level analysis is efficient than packet-level analysis, it is based only on the aggregated details of the flows and meta data. This limits the analysis and would not provide fine-grained details of the traffic. As adversaries are able to blend their malicious content with other legitimate flows, it becomes a challenge to detect anomalous flow-level features. Hence flow-level features are not yet used to identify the malware and other exploits in the encrypted traffic. Graph-based models are also recently gaining attention of the researchers. Zhang et al. [70] have performed the encrypted traffic analysis over byte-level traffic graph through multi-task learning over both packet and flow-level traffic data.

Table 2.6 Flow-based features

S. no	Flow features	Description
1.	Destination port	Port number of the receiver
2.	Flow duration	The total flow duration record
3.	Total Fwd packets	Total number of packets from sender to receiver
4.	Total Bwd packets	Total number of packets from receiver to sender
5.	Total length of Fwd packets	Total size of packets from sender to receiver
6.	Total length of Bwd packets	Total size of packets from receiver to sender
7.	Fwd packet length max	Maximum size of the packet from sender to receiver
8.	Fwd packet length min	Minimum size of the packet from sender to receiver
9.	Fwd packet length mean	Mean size of the packet from sender to receiver
10.	Fwd packet length std	Standard deviation size of the packet from sender to receiver
11.	Bwd packet length max	Maximum size of the packet from receiver to sender
12.	Bwd packet length min	Minimum size of the packet from receiver to sender
13.	Bwd packet length mean	Mean size of the packet from receiver to sender
14.	Bwd packet length std	Standard deviation size of the packet from receiver to sender
15.	Flow bytes/s	Number of flow in bytes per second
16.	Flow packets/s	Number of flow in packets per second
17.	Flow IAT mean	Mean time between two packets sent in the flow
18.	Flow IAT std	Standard deviation time between two packets sent in the flow
19.	Flow IAT max	Maximum time between two packets sent in the flow
20.	Flow IAT min	Minimum time between two packets sent in the flow
21.	Fwd IAT total	Total time between two packets sent from sender to receiver
22.	Fwd IAT mean	Mean time between two packets sent from sender to receiver
23.	Fwd IAT std	Standard deviation time between two packets sent from sender to receiver
24.	Fwd IAT max	Maximum time between two packets sent from sender to receiver
25.	Fwd IAT min	Minimum time between two packets sent from sender to receiver
26.	Bwd IAT total	Total time between two packets sent from receiver to sender
27.	Bwd IAT mean	Mean time between two packets sent from receiver to sender
28.	Bwd IAT std	Standard deviation time between two packets sent from receiver to sender
29.	Bwd IAT max	Maximum time between two packets sent from receiver to sender
30.	Bwd IAT min	Minimum time between two packets sent from receiver to sender

(continued)

Table 2.6 (continued)

S. no	Flow features	Description
31.	Fwd PSH flags	Number of times the PSH flag set to 1 (TCP) and 0 (UDP) for the packets from source to destination
32.	Bwd PSH flags	Number of times the PSH flag set to 1 (TCP) and 0 (UDP) for the packets from destination to source
33.	Fwd URG flags	Number of times the URG flag set to 1 (TCP) and 0 (UDP) for the packets from source to destination
34.	Bwd URG flags	Number of times the PSH flag set to 1 (TCP) and 0 (UDP) for the packets from destination to source
35.	Fwd header length	Total bytes used for packet header from source to destination
36.	Bwd header length	Total bytes used for packet header from destination to source
37.	Fwd packets/s	Number of packets from source to destination per second
38.	Bwd packets/s	Number of packets from destination to source per second
39.	Min packet length	Lower limit on length of a packet
40.	Max packet length	Upper limit on length of a packet
41.	Packet length mean	Mean length of a packet
42.	Packet length Std	Standard deviation length of a packet
43.	Packet length variance	Variance length of a packet
44.	Fin flag count	Number of packets with request for connection termination
45.	Syn flag count	Number of packets in first step of connection establishment phase
46.	RST flag count	Number of packets ready to terminate the connection
47.	PSH flag count	Number of packets with request for immediate delivery
48.	ACK flag count	Number of initial packets successfully received
49.	URG flag count	Number of packets with urgent pointer field
50.	CWR flag count	Number of packets with congestion window reduced flag
51.	ECE flag count	Number of packets received with CE bit set
52.	Down/up ratio	Download and upload ratio
53.	Avg packet size	Average size of packet
54.	Avg Fwd segment size	Average size of the segment from source to destination
55.	Avg Bwd segment size	Average size of the segment from destination to source
56.	Fwd header length	Total bytes used for headers from source to destination
57.	Bwd header length	Total bytes used for headers from destination to source
58.	Fwd Avg bytes/bulk	Average number of bytes in bulk rate from source to destination
59.	Fwd Avg packets/bulk	Average number of packets in bulk rate from source to destination
60.	Fwd Avg bulk rate	Average number of bulk rate from source to destination
61.	Bwd Avg bytes/bulk	Average number of bytes in bulk rate from destination to source
62.	Bwd Avg packets/bulk	Average number of packets in bulk rate from destination to source
63.	Bwd Avg bulk rate	Average number of bulk rate from destination to source

(continued)

Table 2.6 (continued)

S. no	Flow features	Description
64.	Subflow Fwd packets	Average number of packets in a subflow from source to destination
65.	Subflow Fwd bytes	Average number of bytes in a subflow from source to destination
66.	Subflow Bwd packets	Average number of packets in a subflow from destination to source
67.	Subflow Bwd bytes	Average number of bytes in a subflow from destination to source
68.	Init-win-bytes-forward	Total number of bytes sent in initial window from source to destination
69.	Init-win-bytes-backward	Total number of bytes sent in initial window from destination to source
70.	Act-data-pkt-fwd	Count of packets with at least one byte of TCP data payload from source to destination
71.	Min-seg-size-forward	Minimum segment size observed from source to destination
72.	Active mean	Mean time a flow was active before becoming idle
73.	Active std	Standard deviation time a flow was active before becoming idle
74.	Active max	Maximum time a flow was active before becoming idle
75.	Active min	Minimum time a flow was active before becoming idle
76.	Idle mean	Mean time a flow was idle before becoming active
77.	Idle std	Standard deviation time a flow was idle before becoming active
78.	Idle max	Maximum time a flow was idle before becoming active
79.	Idle min	Minimum time a flow was idle before becoming active

2.5.2 Session-Based Features

Session-based features provide more insights beyond packet-based features and are extracted at the flow session level [71]. They provide more inference about the applications than packet-based and flow-based features. Session duration, session size, session timings, session protocols, etc. of unencrypted and encrypted traffic significantly differ. Hence these features help to distinguish the traffic. These features are generally extracted from the network traffic exchanged between the communicating nodes during the period of a session over an encrypted channel. Further, each traffic flow record is first divided into multiple flow points. Then points are aggregated into sessions. There are multiple approaches to this aggregation [8]. Other than sessions established between communicating nodes, traffic flows are organised into multiple sessions. This helps understand complete network events by analysing traffic from relevant or similar or adjacent traffic flows. For this purpose, flow-based information is divided and then aggregated into sessions. Such sessions are formed based on timing or clustering [8]. From these sessions different features can be extracted. Table 2.7 summarises session-based features.

Table 2.7 Session-based features

S. no	Feature	Description
1	Packet size distribution	Size of packets exchanged during a session. This varies with different traffic types; e.g. video traffic has large packets and text-based traffic has smaller packets
2	Inter-packet arrival time	Time between exchange of packets during a session
3	Session duration	Flow duration of each session
4	Total bytes	Total bytes of each session
5	Average duration of flows	Shows the average of the duration of multiple flows
6	Count of flows	Presents the total flows of a session

Table 2.8 Host-based features

S. no	Feature	Description
1.	Key exchange	Key exchange details from the handshake
2.	Certificates	Certificate exchanged during the handshake
3.	Host behaviour	Observations from the host behaviour for fingerprinting. This can be traced from the logs such as applications operations, equipment operations
4.	Host connections	Number of connections host is having
5.	Resource consumption	Resources of the host such as CPU and memory
6.	Opened ports	Ports that are open in the host

2.5.3   Host-Based Features

Host-based features provide insights about the host activities and are collected from the hosts rather than from network. During the handshake, hosts exchange the keys. By analysing the key exchange process, it is possible to identify the kind of encryption used, algorithms involved, etc. Further, during the handshake hosts exchange their digital certificates for authentication. Hence certificate analysis provide insights about endpoints and verify their authenticity. Behavioural patterns of the hosts provide insights to identify the encrypted network traffic. Metadata of the encrypted files provide details of the type of encryption, algorithms involved. Applications and processes running on the endpoints also provide hints about the encrypted traffics that the hosts generate. Hence endpoint security analysis is also essential. Some of the host-based features are listed in Table 2.8. Jing et al. [66] have provided a detailed analysis on the host-based features. Connection-based features and host-based features are summarised in Tables 2.8 and 2.9. Session contains different multiple flows between the communicating nodes as it deals with complete interaction. Other than the classical features, there are contextual flow

Table 2.9 Connection-based features

S. no	Feature	Description
1.	Inbound packets	Number of inbound packets during a particular connection
2.	Outbound packets	Number of outgoing packets during a particular connection
3.	No. of flows	Aggregated number of packet flows during a connection
4.	Average duration	Average duration of a connection
5.	Standard deviation of duration	Standard deviation of connection duration
6.	Ratio of sizes	Ratio of the bytes sent by the receiver to all the bytes transmitted during a connection

features which are extracted from the metadata of the DNS responses, HTTP headers and TLS headers [72].

Extracting relevant features from the traffic data is a challenging task. This is due to the fact that these features are latent and hence cannot directly be inspected. Literature has several approaches to this challenge. These approaches include statistical analysis of the features, cryptographic analysis of the traffic properties, i.e. type of encryption algorithm, length of the key used, etc. Crypto analysis helps to infer the potential information about the payload. Similarly there are ML algorithms to analyse the traffic and extract patterns and features in the traffic [7]. Wang and Thing [73] proposed a traffic feature creation approach to mitigate the issue of non-availability of features specific to encrypted traffic. They have extracted 78 packet-based features and session-based features that are specific to encrypted traffic. They have used RNN models for temporal features, CNN models for payload-based side channel features and classical ML for protocol agnostic features. Subsequently, an ensemble method is applied to obtain the final result.

Feature selection helps in identifying relevant features and removes irrelevant features so that accuracy and efficiency of analysis are improved. Based on the goal and objectives of the analysis, potential features should be identified and irrelevant features should be removed. For example. When the analysis is aimed at certain protocol-based traffic, other protocol types can be removed. Similarly redundant features can be removed by performing correlation analysis. This will improve efficiency and effectiveness of the analysis. Features can be represented in both nominal and numerical data items. Iglesias and Zseby [67] have worked on ranking and selecting the network traffic features based on their contribution to anomaly detection. KDD Cup 99 has 41 features. Among them, the literature has identified 22 features based on the type of attack. NSC-KDD dataset also has 41 features [45]. Different works have identified different feature subsets, when the task is to detect anomaly [16, 36, 65]. The rationality behind such differences among the feature subsets is due to different reasons. These include objectives of the work to be carried out listed in the beginning of this chapter; distribution of data/attacks: the dataset may contain different attack types but they are differently distributed; strong or weak correlation among the features: based on the research objectives, classifiers may look at either for strong correlation or for weak correlation.

Analysis of different varieties of features allows the models to derive many useful inferences about the network traffic. Domain experts select the features and subsequently they are extracted from the traffic data. DL-based feature selections are non-intuitive and avoid human errors. These techniques directly extract the features from the raw traffic data. CNN techniques can even help in predicting the statistical features of the flow from few sample packets from large unlabelled data. RNN models can capture both spatial and temporal features of the flow. Using generative AI techniques such as Generative Adversarial Networks (GAN), synthetic network traffic data can be generated [74].

2.6 Techniques for ENTA

Techniques that work by inspecting the payload are called deep packet inspection (DPI) modes. They are generally used for unencrypted traffic data. Payload-based network traffic classification tools use regular expression matching algorithms. For encrypted traffic, information above layer 4 can be exploited for classification. This include TLS handshake packets that contain plain text data.

Knowledge-based methods create an inference engine using different models such as rule-based models, similarity-based models and signature-based models. Signature-based models available in the literature can be categorised into three groups based on the signatures they generate. They are static signature-based models, dynamic signature-based models and behaviour-based signature models. Traditional protection mechanisms such as firewalls, intrusion prevention systems and intrusion detection systems offer the protection to the resources from the security risks and malicious actors. These mechanisms monitor the network traffic and inspect it for any malicious activities. If they identify any such malicious activity, then they blacklist the nodes. This decision is taken based on inspecting the byte sequences known as signatures [75]. However, signature-based schemes have inherent limitation that they provide protection based on the known signatures and fail to recognise newly emerging attack variants. Overall, knowledge-based methods have inherent limitations such as dependencies on the completeness of the knowledge base. Further, adversaries create content that is normal during the inspection. Detection of anomalies is based on IP address and port numbers. However, there can be an inherent limitation due to the current dynamic nature of IP and port allocations.

Machine learning techniques can be leveraged to analyse different features such as packet and flow to identify anomalies in the network. Selection of ML techniques is based on the objective of the analysis and availability of the data. Unsupervised clustering techniques can group the traffic flows that have similar characteristics. Supervised techniques such as SVM, Decision Trees and Random Forests can be leveraged to classify the network traffic flows. Deep neural network techniques such as CNN and RNN can be leveraged to learn the features from the traffic, classify the network traffic and traffic flows using various traffic features. ML/DL techniques on flow-based features are proved to be effective in detecting malicious network traffic, encrypted malwares, etc. Table 2.10 summarises different techniques used for ENTA.

Table 2.10 Techniques used for ENTA

S. no	Technique	Description
Knowledge-based methods		
1.	Rule based	These methods work based on the prior knowledge obtained about the network traffic and encoded in the form of a knowledge base. Then an inference engine is applied to analyse the knowledge base. These methods are generally highly interpretable. But, due to several limitations, these methods are not generally preferred
2.	Similarity based	
Information theoretic methods [76]		
1.	Entropy based	By measuring the entropy of data distribution in the traffic flow data, anomalous behaviour of the network traffic can be observed. Encrypted network traffic exhibits higher entropy values. Hence these techniques help in detecting encrypted traffic
2.	Parameterised entropy	
3.	Bi-entropy	
Statistical methods [76, 77]		
1.	Pearson correlation	Traffic counts, statistical values of the traffic features, statistical properties of protocols, flows and applications are analysed using different statistical methods
2.	KL divergence	
3.	Distance-based methods	
4.	Parametric and nonparametric models	
Supervised machine learning [6, 7, 65, 78]		
1.	Random forests	These techniques are used for classification when the labels for historical traffic are available. Due to the dependence on the ground truth, models are reliable and model training is easy
2.	Decision trees	
3.	Support vector machines	
4.	Decision trees	
5.	Bayes classifier	
6.	C4.5	
7.	K-NN	
Unsupervised machine learning [6, 7, 79]		
1.	K-means	These techniques deal with the network traffic samples that have no ground truth data
2.	Markov models	
3.	DBSCAN	
4.	XGBoost	
Deep learning [80–82]		
1.	CNN	DL models receive raw traffic as input and learn the features automatically. CNNs can be used to create statistical features of the flow and also to classify. RNNs can capture both spatial and temporal features of the flow. By modelling traffic as graph, it can be combined with graph neural networks (GNN) to analyse the hidden information and classification. Exploiting the correlations between traffic packets, LSTMs can capture the temporal features of packet sequence. Further, transformer-based models with attention-based mechanisms coupled with semi-supervised frameworks can extract features from flow sequences
2.	RNN	
3.	LSTM	
4.	DeepMAL: CNN-LSTM model	
5.	Graph neural networks (GNN)	
6.	Autoencoders	
7.	Transfer learning	
8.	Transformer models	

Statistical techniques such as time-series analysis, correlation analysis, probability models and hypothesis testing can also be used for ENTA. Time series analysis can analyse the regular and irregular time series traffic patterns and identify potential malicious activities. Correlation-based techniques help in understanding and analysing the relationships among the different flow-based features. Hypothesis testing models help in understanding the significance of differences between flow-based features of different traffic types. Statistical techniques have more generalisation ability to any encryption algorithm than intelligent techniques. Probabilistic models such as hidden Markov model (HMM) and entropy-based information theoretic model used to analyse the behaviour of the traffic flows. Information theoretic techniques such as Shannon entropy and bi-entropy help in the ENTA. Typically, encrypted data exhibit entropy values close to 1. So, higher entropy values indicate the presence of encryption in traffic. Training based on bi-entropy over different sets of executable file types provides expected entropy ranges. Hence the malware executables entropy is compared against the expected entropy of normal executables to determine the presence of malware or malicious communications in the encrypted traffic.

Though ML/DL techniques are proved to be outstanding, in classifying the traffic, there are challenges such as sampling and scalability [83]. One of the challenges with ML techniques is the high false positive rate. Recently, there are efforts in the literature in mitigating such issues with ML techniques and optimise the model's performance. Xu et al. [78] have proposed evidence-based verification on top of the ML outcome. If the traffic flow is classified as suspicious flow, then the model would interact with the user. By submitting the outcome as evidence to user, the model seeks the session key. Upon verification, the user can provide the key to the model, to decrypt the flow and verify the traffic content. Lichy et al. [71] have provided a comprehensive comparative analysis on the performance of classical ML and DL models for encrypted malicious traffic classification. Their analysis have proved that ML-based models are performing equally well as DL-based models in binary classification of malware traffic and also multi-class classification of malware families. They have considered Random Forest, Decision Trees, k-NN, M1CNN, M2CNN, DeepMal and MalDIST models. They have also curated three new datasets called MTA B, USTC B and MUB by considering malware and benign samples from different available datasets. Hong et al. [80] have addressed some of the issues with feature-based malicious traffic detection methods. They have proposed a graph-based approach in which encrypted sessions are considered as nodes, features are regarded as attributes of these nodes and then a kNN graph is constructed based on similarity of features. Wang and Thing [73] have provided a two-layer framework that contains ML and DL algorithms to detect encrypted malicious traffic. Even ML and DL techniques can be applied for feature analysis and selection. Shekhawat et al. [65] have demonstrated that feature-related analysis can be performed directly by ML models instead of human experts. Malekghaini et al. [84] have designed a novel tool that can automatically design neural network solutions for encrypted traffic classification. They have designed their model for near real-time classification. For this purpose, they have considered the first three packets of

TLS handshake. They have also provided pointers to the various other research works related to automatic generation of classifiers for network traffic.

Performance of the ENTA solutions that are built based on different techniques, i.e. supervised, unsupervised, etc. analysed based on the criteria such as effectiveness, overhead time and generalisation ability. Performance of any ML/DL technique would be based on the training process and the data used for training the model. There are different validation methods to arrange the data for model training and testing [7]. Performance of the techniques is generally evaluated with the help of classification-related metrics such as true positives, false positives, true positive rate (TPR), false positive rate (FPR), standard deviation (TPR), standard deviation (FPR), precision, recall, accuracy, standard deviation (accuracy), classification time, F-measure, time for model training and testing, time for detection, memory and processor consumption, receiver operating characteristic-area under RoC curve (ROC-AUC), root relative squared error (RRSE) and battery consumption. Also other metrics such as receiver operating characteristic (ROC) curve, area under RoC curve (AUC) and precision-recall curve (P-R curve) are also used to measure the performance of the ENTA techniques. Literature has reported experimental analysis and accuracy of the various techniques with different datasets and features. It is observed that accuracy of the techniques improves with selection of suitable and relevant feature sets. Also when the features do not have a clear variation between malicious and non-malicious traffic, performance of the models is poor. Experiments can be conducted on single feature set or multiple feature sets.

In spite of these developments, there are still challenges and problems in ENTA that need robust solutions. These include creating and curating datasets with variety of samples, feature selection, traffic representation and data imbalance problems, novel techniques with generalisation ability. Very recently Chen et al. [85] have proposed a novel key feature fusion detection method based on generative adversarial network to restore the internal features that are destroyed during the encryption process. This regeneration helps the encrypted traffic detection and classification. Jiang et al. [76] have fused the flow features and path signatures to translate into traffic paths. These paths are analysed by their statistical features and ML techniques. Handling noisy data and labels is another important and challenging task [74]. Further, there should be more robust and secure solutions that are countermeasures to prevent malicious actors in exploiting ENTA for malicious applications. Current ENTA models work with a fixed number of traffic categories and analysis in a centralised node. However, in practical scenarios this working should be scaled up to considering dynamic and different new categories of the traffic that emerge in real time. Also, the analysis should be conducted in a distributed way involving multiple monitoring and analysis nodes. Zhang et al. [86] have proposed a detection method that can adopt to these requirements. Lightweight models for traffic inspection and also feature engineering are gaining attention of the researchers with an aim to increase the traffic analysis efficiency and accuracy [82, 87]. Real-time detection of malicious communication is a huge challenge [74]. We believe that future works on these above directions would make ENTA models more robust, accurate and applicable for real-time traffic.

2.7 Conclusions

Network traffic analysis is important and vital not only for network management tasks but also for security. However, the analysis becomes complex and challenging when the traffic is encrypted. This chapter has provided a detailed analysis on Encrypted Network Traffic Analysis (ENTA). This chapter systematically introduced various stages involved in ENTA including identifying the objectives and purpose of performing traffic analysis, collection of relevant data and processing it, feature selection and extraction, techniques for ENTA and performance analysis of the ENTA. Further, this chapter has also provided several datasets publicly available. Also different sets of features being used in ENTA are discussed. Some of the features are intrinsic to the data and some are derived features. Analysis of features using different techniques such as statistical, intelligent and information theoretic techniques helps to derive inferences about the traffic. Though there is a significant progress in ENTA, there are several challenges as threats are continuously evolving due to the dynamic nature of the traffic. Zero-day classification is a much more challenging task in ENTA. These are the traffic classes that emerge after training of the detection models. It is estimated that 60% of the flows of network traffic are zero-day. Hence there is a wide scope for working on the models that address these problems. The present analysis on the flow-based features is generally conducted on the first few packets of the flow. However, analysis can happen even with the packets from middle of the flow. There are several other challenges related to handling of data, ML models, etc. that need attention of the researchers.

References

1. https://transparencyreport.google.com/https/overview?hl=en
2. Khraisat, A., Gondal, I., Vamplew, P., & Kamruzzaman, J. (2019). Survey of intrusion detection systems: Techniques, datasets and challenges. *Cybersecurity, 2*(1), 1–22.
3. Velan, P., Čermák, M., Čeleda, P., & Drašar, M. (2015). A survey of methods for encrypted traffic classification and analysis. *International Journal of Network Management, 25*(5), 355–374.
4. Zhao, J., Jing, X., Yan, Z., & Pedrycz, W. (2021). Network traffic classification for data fusion: A survey. *Information Fusion, 72*, 22–47.
5. Papadogiannaki, E., & Ioannidis, S. (2021). A survey on encrypted network traffic analysis applications, techniques, and countermeasures. *ACM Computing Surveys (CSUR), 54*(6), 1–35.
6. Wang, Z., Fok, K. W., & Thing, V. L. (2022). Machine learning for encrypted malicious traffic detection: Approaches, datasets and comparative study. *Computers & Security, 113*, 102542.
7. Shen, M., Ye, K., Liu, X., Zhu, L., Kang, J., Yu, S., Li, Q., & Xu, K. (2022). Machine learning-powered encrypted network traffic analysis: A comprehensive survey. *IEEE Communications Surveys & Tutorials., 25*, 791.
8. Feng, Y. (2024). *Fine-grained, content-agnostic network traffic analysis for malicious activity detection.*
9. Dimou, P., Fajfer, J., Müller, N., Papadogiannaki, E., Rekleitis, E., & Střasák, F. (2019). Encrypted traffic analysis. In *European Union agency for cybersecurity (ENISA).*

10. So-In, C. (2009). A survey of network traffic monitoring and analysis tools. In *CSE 576m computer system analysis project*. Washington University in St. Louis.
11. https://www.tcpdump.org/
12. https://www.wireshark.org/
13. https://www.nirsoft.net/utils/smsniff.html
14. https://www.qacafe.com/analysis-tools/cloudshark/
15. https://github.com/jpr5/ngrep
16. McGaughey, D., Semeniuk, T., Smith, R., & Knight, S. (2018). A systematic approach of feature selection for encrypted network traffic classification. In *2018 annual IEEE international systems conference (SysCon)* (pp. 1–8). IEEE.
17. https://www.snort.org/
18. https://www.liveaction.com/products/omnipeek/
19. https://zeek.org/
20. https://www.ettercap-project.org/
21. https://suricata.io/
22. https://www.winpcap.org/
23. https://www.nsnam.org/
24. https://www.netacad.com/courses/packet-tracer
25. https://nmap.org/nping/
26. https://ostinato.org/
27. https://www.solarwinds.com/engineers-toolset/use-cases/traffic-generator-wan-killer
28. https://www.apposite-tech.com/products/netropy-network-emulation/
29. https://bittwist.sourceforge.io/
30. https://tcpreplay.appneta.com/
31. Letteri, I., Della Penna, G., Di Vita, L., & Grifa, M. T. (2020, February). MTA-KDD'19: A dataset for malware traffic detection. In *Itasec* (pp. 153–165).
32. Wang, W., Zhu, M., Zeng, X., Ye, X., & Sheng, Y. (2017). Malware traffic classification using convolutional neural network for representation learning. In *2017 international conference on information networking (ICOIN)* (pp. 712–717). IEEE.
33. Draper-Gil, G., Lashkari, A. H., Mamun, M. S. I., & Ghorbani, A. A. (2016). Characterization of encrypted and VPN traffic using time-related. In *Proceedings of the 2nd international conference on information systems security and privacy (ICISSP)* (pp. 407–414).
34. Mamun, M. S. I., Rathore, M. A., Lashkari, A. H., Stakhanova, N., & Ghorbani, A. A. (2016). Detecting malicious urls using lexical analysis. In *Network and system security: 10th international conference, NSS 2016, Taipei, Taiwan, September 28–30, 2016, Proceedings 10* (pp. 467–482). Springer International Publishing.
35. Abdul Kadir, A. F., Stakhanova, N., & Ghorbani, A. A. (2015). Android botnets: What urls are telling us. In *Network and system security: 9th international conference, NSS 2015, New York, NY, USA, November 3–5, 2015, Proceedings 9* (pp. 78–91). Springer International Publishing.
36. Beigi, E. B., Jazi, H. H., Stakhanova, N., & Ghorbani, A. A. (2014). Towards effective feature selection in machine learning-based botnet detection approaches. In *2014 IEEE conference on communications and network security* (pp. 247–255). IEEE.
37. Habibi Lashkari, A., Kaur, G., & Rahali, A. (2020). Didarknet: A contemporary approach to detect and characterize the Darknet traffic using deep image learning. In *2020 the 10th international conference on communication and network security* (pp. 1–13).
38. Mahdavifar, S., Hanafy Salem, A., Victor, P., Razavi, A. H., Garzon, M., Hellberg, N., & Lashkari, A. H. (2021). Lightweight hybrid detection of data exfiltration using DNS based on machine learning. In *2021 the 11th international conference on communication and network security* (pp. 80–86).
39. Mahdavifar, S., Maleki, N., Lashkari, A. H., Broda, M., & Razavi, A. H. (2021, October). Classifying malicious domains using DNS traffic analysis. In *2021 IEEE Intl conference on dependable, autonomic and secure computing, International conference on pervasive intelligence and computing, International conference on cloud and big data computing,*

International conference on cyber science and technology congress (DASC/PiCom/CBDCom/CyberSciTech) (pp. 60–67). IEEE.

40. Sharafaldin, I., Lashkari, A. H., Hakak, S., & Ghorbani, A. A. (2019). Developing realistic distributed denial of service (DDoS) attack dataset and taxonomy. In *2019 international Carnahan conference on security technology (ICCST)* (pp. 1–8). IEEE.
41. Sharafaldin, I., Lashkari, A. H., & Ghorbani, A. A. (2018). Toward generating a new intrusion detection dataset and intrusion traffic characterization. *ICISSp, 1*, 108–116.
42. Neto, E. C. P., Dadkhah, S., Ferreira, R., Zohourian, A., Lu, R., & Ghorbani, A. A. (2023). *CICIoT2023: A real-time dataset and benchmark for large-scale attacks in IoT environment.*
43. https://www.unb.ca/cic/datasets/dohbrw-2020.html
44. Ikram, S. T., Cherukuri, A. K., Poorva, B., Ushasree, P. S., Zhang, Y., Liu, X., & Li, G. (2021). Anomaly detection using XGBoost ensemble of deep neural network models. *Cybernetics and Information Technologies, 21*(3), 175–188.
45. Tavallaee, M., Bagheri, E., Lu, W., & Ghorbani, A. A. (2009). A detailed analysis of the KDD CUP 99 data set. In *2009 IEEE symposium on computational intelligence for security and defense applications* (pp. 1–6). IEEE.
46. Shiravi, A., Shiravi, H., Tavallaee, M., & Ghorbani, A. A. (2012). Toward developing a systematic approach to generate benchmark datasets for intrusion detection. *Computers & Security, 31*(3), 357–374.
47. Creech, G., & Hu, J. (2013). A semantic approach to host-based intrusion detection systems using contiguous and discontiguous system call patterns. *IEEE Transactions on Computers, 63*(4), 807–819.
48. Elsayed, M. S., Le-Khac, N. A., & Jurcut, A. D. (2020). InSDN: A novel SDN intrusion dataset. *IEEE Access, 8*, 165263–165284.
49. http://www.takakura.com/Kyoto_data/
50. Fontugne, R., Borgnat, P., Abry, P., & Fukuda, K. (2010). Mawilab: Combining diverse anomaly detectors for automated anomaly labeling and performance benchmarking. In *Proceedings of the 6th international conference* (pp. 1–12).
51. Li, D., Zhu, Y., & Lin, W. (2017, December). Traffic identification of mobile apps based on variational autoencoder network. In *2017 13th international conference on computational intelligence and security (CIS)* (pp. 287–291). IEEE.
52. Moore, A., Zuev, D., & Crogan, M. (2013). *Discriminators for use in flow-based classification.*
53. Dong, S., Li, Z., Tang, D., Chen, J., Sun, M., & Zhang, K. (2020). Your smart home can't keep a secret: Towards automated fingerprinting of IOT traffic. In *Proceedings of the 15th ACM Asia conference on computer and communications security* (pp. 47–59).
54. Moustafa, N., & Slay, J. (2015). UNSW-NB15: A comprehensive data set for network intrusion detection systems (UNSW-NB15 network data set). In *2015 military communications and information systems conference (MilCIS)* (pp. 1–6). IEEE.
55. Hamza, A., Gharakheili, H. H., Benson, T. A., & Sivaraman, V. (2019). Detecting volumetric attacks on lot devices via SDN-based monitoring of mud activity. In *Proceedings of the 2019 ACM symposium on SDN research* (pp. 36–48).
56. Aceto, G., Ciuonzo, D., Montieri, A., Persico, V., & Pescapé, A. (2019). MIRAGE: Mobile-app traffic capture and ground-truth creation. In *2019 4th international conference on computing, communications and security (ICCCS)* (pp. 1–8). IEEE.
57. Lashkari, A. H., Kadir, A. F. A., Taheri, L., & Ghorbani, A. A. (2018). Toward developing a systematic approach to generate benchmark android malware datasets and classification. In *2018 international Carnahan conference on security technology (ICCST)* (pp. 1–7). IEEE.
58. Hjelmvik, E., & Cert, S. A. F. (2015). Hands-on network forensics. *Swedish Armed Forces CERT FIRST.*
59. Garcia, S., Grill, M., Stiborek, J., & Zunino, A. (2014). An empirical comparison of botnet detection methods. *Computers & Security, 45*, 100–123.

60. Liberatore, M., & Levine, B. N. (2006). Inferring the source of encrypted HTTP connections. In *Proceedings of the 13th ACM conference on computer and communications security* (pp. 255–263).
61. https://www.manageengine.com/products/netflow/
62. Liu, J., Tian, Z., Zheng, R., & Liu, L. (2019). A distance-based method for building an encrypted malware traffic identification framework. *IEEE Access, 7*, 100014–100028.
63. Bazuhair, W., & Lee, W. (2020). Detecting malign encrypted network traffic using Perlin noise and convolutional neural network. In *2020 10th annual computing and communication workshop and conference (CCWC)* (pp. 0200–0206). IEEE.
64. Shekhawat, A. S. (2018). *Analysis of encrypted malicious traffic.*
65. Shekhawat, A. S., Di Troia, F., & Stamp, M. (2019). Feature analysis of encrypted malicious traffic. *Expert Systems with Applications, 125*, 130–141.
66. Jing, X., Yan, Z., & Pedrycz, W. (2018). Security data collection and data analytics in the internet: A survey. *IEEE Communications Surveys & Tutorials, 21*(1), 586–618.
67. Iglesias, F., & Zseby, T. (2015). Analysis of network traffic features for anomaly detection. *Machine Learning, 101*, 59–84.
68. Yoshimura, N., Kuzuno, H., Shiraishi, Y., & Morii, M. (2022). DOC-IDS: A deep learning-based method for feature extraction and anomaly detection in network traffic. *Sensors, 22*(12), 4405.
69. Chen, Z., Cheng, G., Wei, Z., & Niu, D. (2023). Classify traffic rather than flow: Versatile multi-flow encrypted traffic classification with flow clustering. *IEEE Transactions on Network and Service Management, 21*, 1446.
70. Zhang, H., Xiao, X., Yu, L., Li, Q., Ling, Z., & Zhang, Y. (2024). One train for two tasks: An encrypted traffic classification framework using supervised contrastive learning. *arXiv preprint arXiv:2402.07501.*
71. Lichy, A., Bader, O., Dubin, R., Dvir, A., & Hajaj, C. (2023). When a RF beats a CNN and GRU, together—A comparison of deep learning and classical machine learning approaches for encrypted malware traffic classification. *Computers & Security, 124*, 103000.
72. Anderson, B., & McGrew, D. (2016). Identifying encrypted malware traffic with contextual flow data. In *Proceedings of the 2016 ACM workshop on artificial intelligence and security* (pp. 35–46).
73. Wang, Z., & Thing, V. L. (2023). Feature mining for encrypted malicious traffic detection with deep learning and other machine learning algorithms. *Computers & Security, 128*, 103143.
74. Moure-Garrido, M., Campo, C., & Garcia-Rubio, C. (2023). Real time detection of malicious DoH traffic using statistical analysis. *Computer Networks, 234*, 109910.
75. Yang, J., & Lim, H. (2021). Deep learning approach for detecting malicious activities over encrypted secure channels. *IEEE Access, 9*, 39229–39244.
76. Jiang, C., Xu, S., Geng, G., Weng, J., & Zhang, X. (2023). Seq2Path: A sequence-to-path-based flow feature fusion approach for encrypted traffic classification. *Cluster Computing, 26*(3), 1785–1800.
77. Hazelton, M. L. (2014). Statistical methods in network traffic. In *Wiley StatsRef: Statistics reference online* (pp. 1–6).
78. Xu, B., He, G., & Zhu, H. (2021). ME-box: A reliable method to detect malicious encrypted traffic. *Journal of Information Security and Applications, 59*, 102823.
79. Zhou, Z., Bin, H., Li, J., Yin, Y., Chen, X., Ma, J., & Yao, L. (2022). Malicious encrypted traffic features extraction model based on unsupervised feature adaptive learning. *Journal of Computer Virology and Hacking Techniques, 18*(4), 453–463.
80. Hong, Y., Li, Q., Yang, Y., & Shen, M. (2023). Graph based encrypted malicious traffic detection with hybrid analysis of multi-view features. *Information Sciences, 644*, 119229.
81. Zhou, Y., Shi, H., Zhao, Y., Ding, W., Han, J., Sun, H., Zhang, X., Tang, C., & Zhang, W. (2023). Identification of encrypted and malicious network traffic based on one-dimensional convolutional neural network. *Journal of Cloud Computing, 12*(1), 1–10.

82. Zhao, R., Deng, X., Yan, Z., Ma, J., Xue, Z., & Wang, Y. (2022). MT-FlowFormer: A semi-supervised flow transformer for encrypted traffic classification. In *Proceedings of the 28th ACM SIGKDD conference on knowledge discovery and data mining* (pp. 2576–2584).
83. Kattadige, C., Choi, K. N., Wijesinghe, A., Nama, A., Thilakarathna, K., Seneviratne, S., & Jourjon, G. (2021). SETA++: Real-time scalable encrypted traffic analytics in multi-Gbps networks. *IEEE Transactions on Network and Service Management, 18*(3), 3244–3259.
84. Malekghaini, N., Akbari, E., Salahuddin, M. A., Limam, N., Boutaba, R., Mathieu, B., Moteau, S., & Tuffin, S. (2023). AutoML4ETC: Automated neural architecture search for real-world encrypted traffic classification. *IEEE Transactions on Network and Service Management.*
85. Chen, F., Bai, J., & Gao, W. (2023). Research on encrypted traffic detection based on key features. *IEEE Access, 12*, 1786.
86. Zhang, P., Chen, F., & Yue, H. (2024). Detection and utilization of new-type encrypted network traffic in distributed scenarios. *Engineering Applications of Artificial Intelligence, 127*, 107196.
87. Liu, Q., Peng, Y., Jiang, H., Wu, J., Wang, T., Peng, T., & Wang, G. (2022). SlimBox: Lightweight packet inspection over encrypted traffic. *IEEE Transactions on Dependable and Secure Computing., 20*, 4359.

Chapter 3
Classification of Encrypted Network Traffic

3.1 Introduction

Encrypted traffic is permitted in most organisations so that secure transactions such as Internet banking can be performed by employees. In such cases, the organisations can mistakenly allow anomalous traffic or unauthorised traffic in masquerade consisting of unauthorised protocols, prohibited websites or malicious file categories. It is impossible to overlook encrypted network traffic categorisation because of their growing volume. Wright et al. [1] analysed the popularity of encrypted protocols and inferred that there have been advancements in network security but with trade-offs in cost and time. A number of approaches for encrypted traffic categorisation are available in the literature [2–5]. Encrypted traffic categorisation, whether normal or abnormal, results in many challenges if the transferred data is misrepresented by muddling the port numbers and protocols. It is ineffective to block IP addresses and port numbers as most destabilising and commercial applications intentionally utilise non-standard ports to bypass firewalls [6].

Recent research has focused on developing a general purpose approach to identify feature subsets for encrypted traffic categorisation [7]. Machine learning approaches can result in augmenting the less capable classifier with the given training data to categorise unseen information [8]. Various machine learning-based approaches are detailed in the next chapter.

This chapter presents in detail various approaches to encrypted traffic classification for specific applications and the feature selection adopted for efficient traffic classification.

© The Author(s), under exclusive license to Springer Nature Switzerland AG 2024
A. K. Cherukuri et al., *Encrypted Network Traffic Analysis*, SpringerBriefs in Computer Science, https://doi.org/10.1007/978-3-031-62909-9_3

3.2 Methods for Encrypted Traffic Classification

Traffic flow classification can be analysed using three essential factors: (1) port, (2) deep packet inspection (DPI) and (3) flow.

3.2.1 Port-Based Approach

The first factor based on port requires TCP or UDP port values for categorising online applications. The port-based approach is widely used either separately or in tandem with other attributes. It is inaccurate and suited only for unencrypted traffic classification and has a high computational overhead [9]. Table 3.1 shows the basic five features required for port-based classification which is also used in other approaches.

3.2.2 Deep Packet Inspection

Traditional packet analysis tools scan the packets at the IP and TCP layers, whereas DPI approach scans the application layer to identify whether there is any virus, spam or intrusion and deploy preventive measures subsequently. Therefore, it is also known as payload-based analysis. DPI has better performance in comparison to port number. The payload data is mined using regular expressions or string search [10] to check the state of the packet. In addition, Wireshark tool [11] can be used with open source nDPI project [12] to characterise the packet records. Figure 3.1 shows the packet filtering process using DPI. Filtering rules are applied at all layers from physical to application layer [13]. The packets are allowed to enter the network only if the rule matches. Otherwise, the packets are dropped. The application layer protocol can be considered as the Real-Time Transport (RTP) protocol if DPI is utilised. Figure 3.2 shows the pattern recognition process deployed in DPI by integrating several techniques such as flow tracking, pattern matching and statistical analysis. However, DPI is inaccurate as it cannot directly decrypt data for traffic using encryption protocols. A shared or arbitrator key [14] is required to decrypt

Table 3.1 Basic features for port-based approach

Feature	Description
Srcip	Sender IP address
Srcport	Sender port number
Dstnip	Target IP address
Dstnport	Target port number
Prt	Protocol

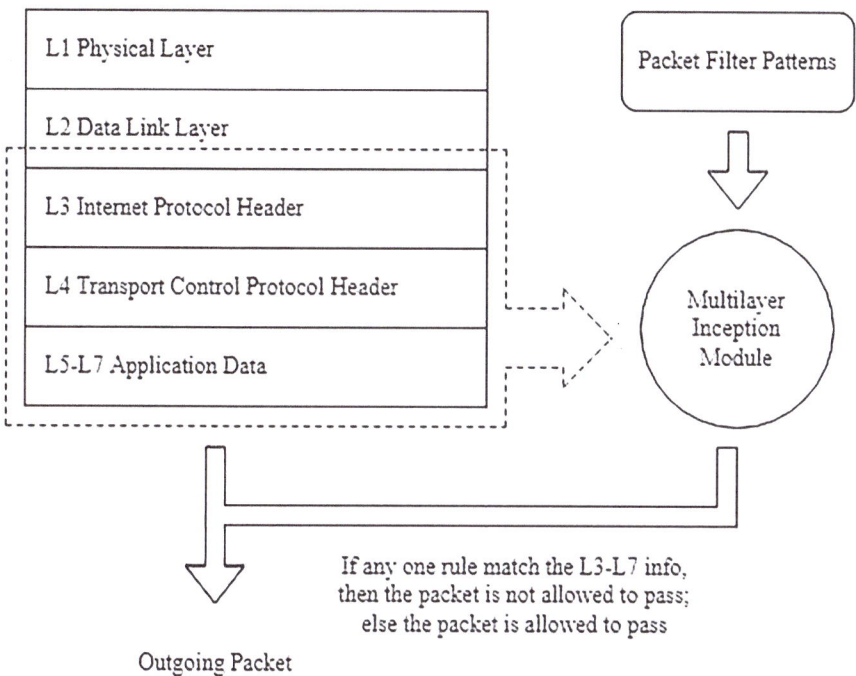

Fig. 3.1 Packet filtering in DPI

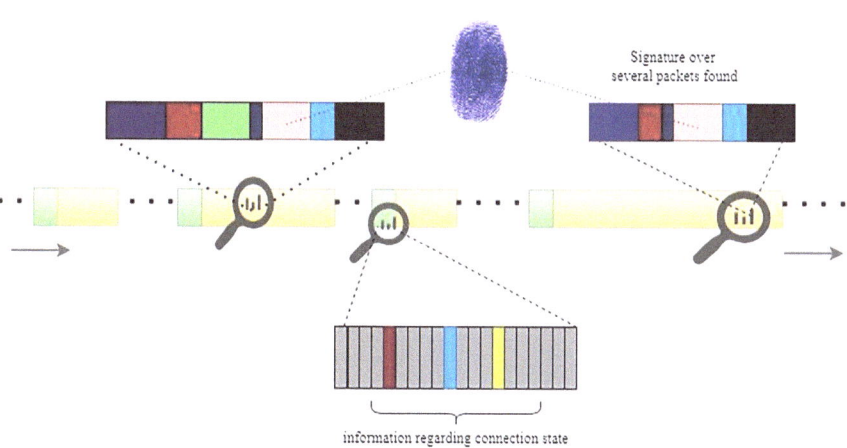

Fig. 3.2 Pattern recognition in DPI

data and perform traffic detection which can be dangerous to data privacy and security. Thus, the limitation with payload technique is that encrypted traffic cannot be analysed. The other disadvantage of DPI is computational overhead, and therefore it cannot be used in mission critical systems [2–4].

3.2.3   Time-Based Features

Common attributes derived from temporal features are size of the packet along with the direction (request or response) and inter-arrival time. These attributes can differentiate various network traffic categories [15], and multiple packet attributes can be analysed. Table 3.2 shows the temporal features which are used in single- and multiple-flow approaches. It is based on a single direction or bidirectional traffic request and response. Statistical attributes such as mean and standard deviation in the forward and reverse direction are also aggregated temporal features. A burst is a type of accumulation, wherein the packet sequence is directed in the request path and is present among the packets sent in the response path [16]. Therefore, the burst time and size are beneficial. A surge period is another aggregation done on the channel-transmitting packets in request or response direction continuously. The initial "m" constituents of wavelet transformations utilise these attributes to determine whether the end user is accessing the website by a tunnelled VPN.

3.2.4   Single and Multiple Flow-Based Approaches

Single flow-based network traffic classification is analysed in most studies [17]. A single flow comprises 5-tuple data namely the protocol, source port, destination port, source and destination address. Gezer [17] analysed the single flow-based

Table 3.2 Temporal features utilised for classification

Feature	Description
Time	Flow time
AIT	Avg. packet arrival period
BPS	The average bits-per-second
PPS	Total packets sent per second
FPH	Total flows per hour
MiFIP	Minimum frontward inter-arrival period
MiRIP	Minimum reverse inter-arrival period
SFIP	Std deviation of frontward inter-arrival period
SRIP	Std deviation of reverse inter-arrival period
MFIP	Mean frontward inter-arrival period
MRIP	Mean reverse inter-arrival period

attributes such as flow duration, packet length average and number of incoming and outgoing bytes. Korczynski and Duda [18] observed the packet sequence to develop a Markov model. Yang [19] modelled the flow distribution using inter-arrival time of packets and packet size. These single-flow attributes are commonly used in traffic classification methods.

Extraction of attributes from various flows of a sliding time window is considered as multiple flow. A proxy application traffic detection analysed the multiple flow attributes by observing the flow burst in a minimum time window [20]. The attributes are maximum flow burst lengths, total flow burst size and count of flow bursts. Patil [21] integrated single flow-based attributes and few multiple flow-based attributes such as total number of flows with similar source and destination IP address. Thus, multiple flow-based attributes are used in various traffic classification situations for enhancing the traffic performance. The bag of flow (BoF) concept is used in various studies [17–19], and a BoF is defined as a group of flows with the same transport protocol, destination address and destination port which specifies the network traffic sent over time by the same server application on the same port. Yao et al. [22] considered the initial four packets of every flow and ignored other packets, which are applicable in the identification of unseen behaviour in the dataset required for classification.

3.3 Traffic Preprocessing

There is a lack of dependable approaches for network traffic preprocessing [23]. IP whitelisting technology is utilised in most of the effective preprocessing approaches. However, not every whitelist IP obtained from the Internet resource is reliable. AlienVault [24], IBM-XForce Exchange [25] and Recorded Future [26] which are threat intelligence groups offer IP blacklist sources which are used to identify malware but do not provide whitelist information. Therefore, a fast and reliable approach for collecting IP whitelists is necessary.

Zheng et al. [27] preprocessed the packet header and payload separately. The protocol, TCP/UDP port and TCP flags information will be retrieved from the header which in turn will be used for identifying the type of traffic on the transport layer. Also, if the payload size is more than "N" bytes, either truncation or padding to "N" bytes is performed. The data is then normalised to limit to the range [0,1]. The protocol field and the address field are the primary attributes in the network layer. It is important to determine the connecting server IP address based on the traffic direction. The transport layer can send either TCP or UDP traffic. Hence, the common port field of the two is identified as the attribute consisting of source and destination. In general, there are more flag fields in TCP header rather than UDP for transmission control. If it is an UDP packet, it is substituted by zeros. The authors analysed different header attributes to test the impact on accuracy. They concluded that the performance will be high if there are more header attribute values.

3.4   Encrypted Application Traffic Classification

Encrypted traffic categorisation is required by most of the network services in day-to-day life. Encryption techniques are steadily protecting user's privacy but it is to be noted that the traditional approaches are neither able to perform generalisation nor can hardly achieve the accurate performance. In general, the underlying protocols contain traffic components, which are primarily meant for communication control and not application traffic detection. Therefore, it is difficult to differentiate information between applications and categorise them. However, few of the protocol attributes can accomplish application detection as they operate with similar network settings. This is very useful to diversify the traffic based on the port, address and time to live. It is still not dependable to use these fundamental protocol attributes for classification. Figure 3.3 shows the encrypted network traffic classification. In Fig. 3.3, the incoming traffic attributes are analysed and new attributes are calculated from existing attributes to build a dataset. The dataset is then fed to the detective model for training and new traffic is identified as either normal or malicious during testing.

Table 3.3 shows the comparison of related works on encrypted traffic classification. Casino et al. [28] developed an approach named HEDGE which randomly evaluates the payload data and classifies the network traffic into encrypted and compressed traffic. Distinct packet sizes were utilised to train and test their proposed approach. A random packet size of 64 KB produced an accuracy of 94.72% and accuracy less than 70.61% for small packet size. Aouni et al. [29] analysed four

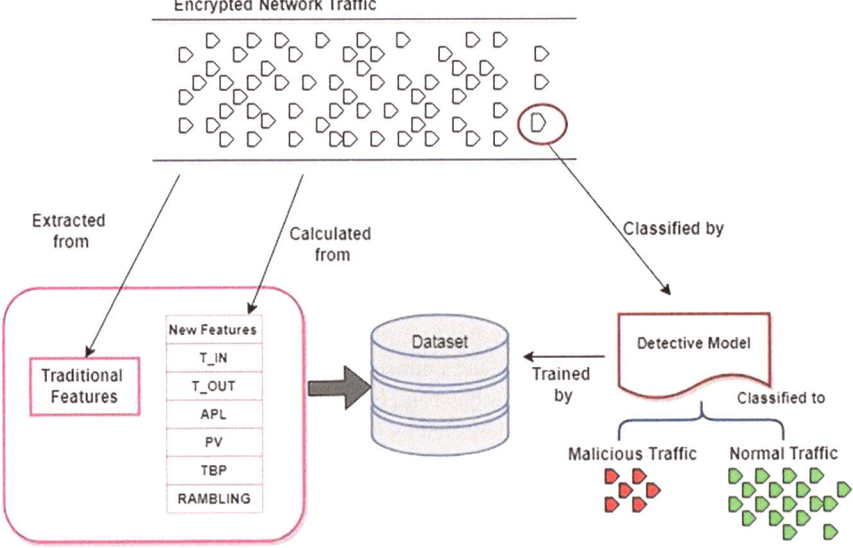

Fig. 3.3 Encrypted Network Traffic Classification using existing and derived attributes

Table 3.3 Comparison of the related works

Paper	Data	Input category	MTU (bytes)	Number of packets per flow	Number of classes	Technique	Task	Results
Casino et al. [28]	Arbitrary encrypted and compressed files	Flow	64 KB	–	2	HEDGE	Encrypted and compressed network traffic categorisation	Acc = 94.72%
Aouini et al. [29]	French ISP residential network	Flow	–	4	7	C5.0	Encrypted network traffic classification	Acc = 98.8%
Miller et al. [30]	VPN non-VPN	Flow & time series	–	–	2	MLP NN	Encrypted VPN network traffic classification	Acc = 94%
Vrana et al. [31]	–	Flow	–	10	–	Hardware	Real-time analysis and monitoring of encrypted network traffic data	NA
Zeng et al. [32]	VPN and non-VPN	Flow & time series	900	–	7	ID-CNN LSTM SAE	Traffic classification and intrusion detection	ID-CNN acc = 99.85% for traffic class. LSTM acc = 99.48% for intrusion identification
Salman et al. [33]	Custom-generated dataset and ISCX TOR-non-TOR ISCX VPN-non-VPN	Session	150	16	4	CNN	Traffic classification	Acc = 95%
Lotfollahi et al [34]	ISCX VPN-non-VPN	IP packets	1500	–	12 classes and 17 applications	ID-CNN-SAE	Traffic classification and application identification	ID-CNN precision = 94% for traffic class. 98% for the application detection
Shapira and Shavitt [35]	ISCX TOR non-TOR VPN-non-VPN	Flow	1500	–	5	CNN	Traffic classification and application identification	Accuracy = 85% for non-VPN traffic

packets from every flow and achieved 98.8% accuracy in categorising network traffic into seven classes. Miller et al. [30] developed a model using Multi-Layered Perceptron (MLP) Neural Network (NN) to identify and categorise inbound Internet traffic generated by OpenVPN. The TCP flows collected using encrypted VPN sessions are monitored along with the other TCP flows gathered during browsing. The model categorised VPN and non-VPN traffic with 94% accuracy using the ten flow-based attributes. Vrana et al. [31] implemented a hardware approach to analyse and observe the encrypted network traffic data by integrating Field Programmable Gate Array (FPGA) logic utilisation and proposed a new approach to extract the attributes of such traffic. The attributes determined are average packet size, packet length, inter-arrival time packets and the n-bit length entropy using the initial ten packets from the flow. Zeng et al. [32] presented a technique called Deep-Full-Range (DFR) for categorising the network traffic and identifying intrusions. The seven types of encrypted network traffic such as web browsing, email, chat, streaming, file transfer, VoIP and P2P are categorised. Salman et al. [33] built a multi-level classification model using deep learning to categorise Internet traffic by observing 16 packets in each flow and subflow with maximum transmission unit (MTU) of 784 bytes from diverse applications and devices. The authors tested their model on encapsulated and encrypted data, and VPN (UNB, 2016) and TOR (UNB, 2017) public datasets were analysed. Encrypted network traffic is classified into four classes (streaming, interactive, bulk data transfer and transaction) with 95.84% accuracy. Lotfollahi et al. [34] developed a Deep Packet model to detect and classify the end-user activities and differentiate the network traffic using deep learning approaches. They utilised UNB 2016 dataset which had 17 categories of applications like Gmail, Netflix and Facebook and 12 activities like streaming, VPN and VoIP. Shapira et al. [35] developed the "FlowPic" approach to classify encrypted traffic by transforming the network flow data, which contains arrival times and packet sizes into an image. Finally, a deep learning classifier is utilised to categorise the traffic flow and determine their applications.

Encrypted traffic classification [36] is performed by integrating payload content and statistics. It is apparent that combining two dimensions is better than considering only one aspect because various applications may behave similarly in one dimension. For instance, email and chat applications act differently in their content but alike in statistics, as they both perform limited transmissions in a time interval. Also, file transfer and torrent applications behave differently in their file content as they have diverse transmissions in two directions. Therefore, these applications are dissimilar statistically. The authors named the framework as comprehensive effective transformation analytics (CETAnalytics). The framework is highly flexible and powerful. Several experiments were conducted using the ISCXVPN2016 dataset. Encrypted traffic identification [37–40] is performed utilising the session statistics and balancing the artificial data generated using Synthetic Minority Over-Sampling Technique (SMOTE). This technique is used to minimise the imbalance in the encrypted traffic classification based on statistical attributes. Thus, using packet header and statistical attributes to differentiate encrypted traffic is effective. Gerard et al. [41] implemented a two-stage classification approach using session attributes and classifiers to categorise different types of business traffic. In this approach, the traffic is first classified into VPN and non-VPN and in the second step, traffic is classified into specific behaviour.

A flow-based approach was developed to categorise encrypted VPN traffic by utilising time-based attributes [42]. The computational overhead is minimised by reducing the attribute set which can be extracted with low computational complexity. In addition, an extensive labelled dataset of encrypted traffic is generated and labelled by 14 various labels. Time-based attributes are only chosen to accelerate the efficiency and to construct an independent traffic classification. Wang et al. [43] built an approach to describe P2P (peer-to-peer) traffic. The attributes are extracted from various flows and combined flows into clusters to retrieve P2P application characteristics. Mamun et al. [44] built an approach to calculate the payload entropy to identify encrypted traffic. Sherry et al. [45] built a DPI to analyse encrypted payload deprived of decrypting it, to ensure the communication secrecy. However, only HTTPS traffic can be analysed. Wei et al. [46] developed a BotMark which performed automated botnet identification with a fusion model of flow- and graph-based traffic attributes wherein an ensemble is performed on identification, similarity, anomaly and stability scores. This model resulted in 99.9% detection accuracy thereby outperforming singular flow-based or graph-based approaches.

Various flow-based approaches are developed for traffic categorisation [47] to guarantee the veracity of traffic flow records from source to destination in an IoT environment. Hashed flow records are sent and also incorporated with symmetric and asymmetric encryption techniques. Wright et al. [37, 48] identified the application protocol by using the connection-based attributes such as packet size, time and direction. They deployed hidden Markov models (HMM) to learn the performance. However, the detection rate (DR) of SSH is only 76%. Palmieri et al. utilised non-linear recurrence plot-based technique accordingly to classify traffic flows using two attributes namely inter-arrival period variance and packet size. A true positive rate (TPR) of 89% is obtained. A profile-based approach is built by Hu et al. [49] which is a bi-level matching technique using host based and flow based to determine P2P flow traffic with PP live and BitTorrent as binary scenarios. Their flow attributes comprise the five flow elements (SourceIP, destnIP, SourcePort, DestnPort and Protocol) and statistical flow attributes. Apriori technique builds a flow behaviour using best association rules and determines their rule sets. An average accuracy of 98 and 97% is obtained for PPlive and BitTorrent over TCP and UDP, respectively [1]. In this case, TPR and FPR are not supported. Most of the literature available is for identifying VoIP traffic such as Skype as it has multiple users logged in at a given time [50]. Due to the dynamic nature of encrypted traffic, Skype analysis is becoming widespread in the past few years. Suh.et al. [50] monitored and classified such Skype traffic using relay nodes which is a fragment of the distributed Skype network. This can easily route the Skype traffic bypassing firewalls and Network Address Translation (NAT). Various metrics were determined using attributes such as inter-arrival period, byte size and highest cross correlation among two transmitted packet bursts to identify Skype traffic. TPR of 96% and FPR of 4% are achieved and the technique can only identify relay Skype sessions. However, all

Skype VoIP traffic cannot be classified by this approach. Robin et al. [51] analysed encrypted traffic of AMI and built an IDS which does not require inspection of packet payload. Similar packets are labelled by using the following attributes such as packet size, packet directions and the comparative packet positioning period. The approach focuses on analysing C12.22 encrypted traffic to identify irregular behaviour. Single-packet flows and bi-packet flows are identified with request-reply sets which helps to create flow-based attribute vectors. These vectors comprise (1) the payload size in the initial packet of the flow, (2) second packet payload size in the flow, (3) the time between packets and (4) flow direction.

A forensic analysis is performed [37] utilising traces gathered from various networks using two encrypted applications such as Skype and Secure Shell (SSH). There is a detection mechanism to find services which are active in encrypted tunnels. A port-based approach is used to label the traces of datasets. The authors label the applications/services executed in various SSH tunnels. Various labels present are (i) SCP which represents a secure copy connection; (ii) SFTP which specifies secure file transfer; (iii) LocalT which represents local machine tunnelling session; (iv) RemoteT which specifies remote machine tunnelling session; (v) X11—representing an X11 session; and (vi) shell which represents remote login connection. A subset sampling is performed to minimise the CPU and memory time essential for training. The sample is generated from random flows of five various applications namely File Transfer Protocol (FTP), Microsoft Notification (MSN), SSH, DNS and HTTP. The authors used 12,246 flows of University of Dalhousie traces. The traffic is divided into equal numbers of SSH and non-SSH flows. The packet header features of the training samples are utilised for SSH tunnel detection. In another case, for identifying Skype traffic, a random sample of Skype traffic is generated and selected from various classes (SSH, FTP, HTTP, DNS and MSN). The training sample of Skype traffic comprises 828,964 flows, wherein 4,72,784 are Skype flows and 3,56,810 are non-Skype flows. Skype tunnel detection is performed using header attributes. Skype training samples are generated by random sampling using an even probability technique. Skype packet headers consist of 6,00,000 balanced packets. In this approach, SSH and Skype encrypted traffic are determined by a data-driven approach. A subset of attributes is retrieved which can result in a robust/generalised practice on real-time network traffic data. Each packet in this analysis consists of 39 attributes. Wireshark is utilised to process the data and generate attributes. In the flow-based attribute set, a feature is considered as a statistic and is calculated from more than one packet for every flow. Nearly 22 attributes are computed after flow generation using Netmate. The flow direction is fixed as forward based on the first packet sent containing only TCP and UDP flows. In addition to academic research, a solution which is adopted in the industry is based on certificates [52]. These certificates use the subject alternative names (SAN) information or the server name indication (SNI) in TLS extension to categorise traffic types which is commonly implemented in the industry. This solution will fail with the adoption of TLS 1.3 for encrypting certificates [52].

3.5 Conclusion

This chapter has detailed the various approaches utilised for classifying encrypted traffic. A detailed literature review is performed on various types of encrypted traffic classification performed using packet-based and flow-based approaches. A comparison of the related works on various encrypted datasets containing VPN and TOR traffic is studied for application traffic classification. In the next chapter, we will discuss the attacks targeting the encrypted protocols and the detection mechanism to trace the attackers and prevention schemes.

References

1. Wright, C. V., Monrose, F., & Masson, G. M. (2006). On inferring application protocol behaviors in encrypted network traffic. *Journal of Machine Learning Research, 7*(12).
2. Bernaille, L., & Teixeira, R. (2007). Early recognition of encrypted applications. In *International conference on passive and active network measurement* (pp. 165–175). Springer.
3. Dusi, M., Crotti, M., Gringoli, F., & Salgarelli, L. (2009). Tunnel hunter: Detecting application-layer tunnels with statistical fingerprinting. *Computer Networks, 53*(1), 81–97.
4. Crotti, M., Dusi, M., Gringoli, F., & Salgarelli, L. (2007). Detecting HTTP tunnels with statistical mechanisms. In *IEEE international conference on communications ICC '07* (pp. 6162–6168).
5. Karagiannis, T., Papagiannaki, K., & Faloutsos, M. (2005). BLINC: Multilevel traffic classification in the dark. In *Proceedings of the 2005 conference on Applications, technologies, architectures, and protocols for computer communications* (pp. 229–240).
6. Erman, J., Mahanti, A., Arlitt, M., Cohen, I., & Williamson, C. (2007). Offline/realtime traffic classification using semi-supervised learning. *Performance Evaluation, 64*(9–12), 1194–1213.
7. McGaughey, D., Semeniuk, T., Smith, R., & Knight, S. (2018). A systematic approach of feature selection for encrypted network traffic classification. In *2018 annual IEEE international systems conference (SysCon)* (pp. 1–8). IEEE.
8. Papadogiannaki, E., & Ioannidis, S. (2021). A survey on encrypted network traffic analysis applications, techniques, and countermeasures. *ACM Computing Surveys (CSUR), 54*(6), 1–35.
9. Ahmed, A. A., & Agunsoye, G. (2021). A real-time network traffic classifier for online applications using machine learning. *Algorithms, 14*(8), 250.
10. Aho, A. V., & Corasick, M. J. (1975). Efficient string matching: An aid to bibliographic search. *Communications of the ACM, 18*(6), 333–340.
11. Wireshark User's Guide, Version 3.3.0. Available online: https://www.wireshark.org/download/docs/user-guide.pdf. Accessed on 15 Mar 2020.
12. Deri, L., Martinelli, M., Bujlow, T., & Cardigliano, A. (2014). ndpi: Open-source high-speed deep packet inspection. In *2014 International wireless communications and mobile computing conference (IWCMC)* (pp. 617–622). IEEE.
13. Cho, Y. H., & Mangione-Smith, W. H. (2008). Deep network packet filter design for reconfigurable devices. *ACM Transactions on Embedded Computing Systems (TECS), 7*(2), 1–26.
14. Say "Yes" to HTTPS: Chrome Secures the Web, One Site at a Time. Available online: https://www.blog.google/technology/safety-security/say-yes-https-chrome-secures-web-one-site-time/. Accessed on 20 Oct 2017.
15. Lu, G., Zhang, H., Qassrawi, M., & Yu, X. (2012). Comparison and analysis of flow features at the packet level for traffic classification. In *2012 international conference on connected vehicles and expo (ICCVE)* (pp. 262–267). IEEE.

16. Shi, Y., & Biswas, S. (2014). Website fingerprinting using traffic analysis of dynamic web-pages. In *2014 IEEE global communications conference* (pp. 557–563). IEEE.

17. Gezer, A., Warner, G., Wilson, C., & Shrestha, P. (2019). A flow-based approach for Trickbot banking trojan detection. *Computers & Security, 84*, 179–192.

18. Korczyński, M., & Duda, A. (2014). Markov chain fingerprinting to classify encrypted traffic. In *IEEE INFOCOM 2014-IEEE conference on computer communications* (pp. 781–789). IEEE.

19. Yang, Y., Kang, C., Gou, G., Li, Z., & Xiong, G. (2018). TLS/SSL encrypted traffic classification with autoencoder and convolutional neural network. In *2018 IEEE 20th international conference on high performance computing and communications; IEEE 16th international conference on Smart City; IEEE 4th international conference on data science and systems (HPCC/SmartCity/DSS)* (pp. 362–369). IEEE.

20. Zeng, X., Chen, X., Shao, G., He, T., Han, Z., Wen, Y., & Wang, Q. (2019). Flow context and host behavior based shadowsocks's traffic identification. *IEEE Access, 7*, 41017–41032.

21. Patil, R., Dudeja, H., & Modi, C. (2019). Designing an efficient security framework for detecting intrusions in virtual network of cloud computing. *Computers & Security, 85*, 402–422.

22. Yao, H., Liu, C., Zhang, P., Wu, S., Jiang, C., & Yu, S. (2019). Identification of encrypted traffic through attention mechanism based long short term memory. *IEEE Transactions on Big Data, 8*(1), 241–252.

23. Huang, Y. F., Lin, C. B., Chung, C. M., & Chen, C. M. (2021). Research on qos classification of network encrypted traffic behavior based on machine learning. *Electronics, 10*(12), 1376.

24. Alienvault, Alienvault, Inc., Alienvault, San Mateo, CA, USA, 2020, https://otx.alienvault.com.

25. IBM X-Force Exchange, IBM Security, IBM X-Force Exchange, Atlanta, GA, USA, 2020., https://exchange.xforce. ibmcloud.com.

26. Recorded Future, Recorded Future, Inc, Recorded Future, Somerville, MA, USA, 2020., https://support.recordedfuture. com.

27. Zheng, R., Liu, J., Niu, W., Liu, L., Li, K., & Liao, S. (2020). Preprocessing method for encrypted traffic based on semisupervised clustering. *Security and Communication Networks, 2020*, 1–13.

28. Casino, F., Choo, K. K. R., & Patsakis, C. (2019). HEDGE: Efficient traffic classification of encrypted and compressed packets. *IEEE Transactions on Information Forensics and Security, 14*(11), 2916–2926.

29. Aouini, Z., Kortebi, A., Ghamri-Doudane, Y., & Cherif, I. L. (2018). Early classification of residential networks traffic using C5. 0 machine learning algorithm. In *2018 wireless days (WD)* (pp. 46–53). IEEE.

30. Miller, S., Curran, K., & Lunney, T. (2018). Multilayer perceptron neural network for detection of encrypted VPN network traffic. In *2018 international conference on cyber situational awareness, data analytics and assessment (cyber SA)* (pp. 1–8). IEEE.

31. Vrána, R., Kořenek, J., & Novák, D. (2019). Acceleration of feature extraction for real-time analysis of encrypted network traffic. In *2019 IEEE 22nd international symposium on design and diagnostics of electronic circuits & systems (DDECS)* (pp. 1–6). IEEE.

32. Zeng, Y., Gu, H., Wei, W., & Guo, Y. (2019). $ deep-full-range $: A deep learning based network encrypted traffic classification and intrusion detection framework. *IEEE Access, 7*, 45182–45190.

33. Salman, O., Elhajj, I. H., Chehab, A., & Kayssi, A. (2018). A multi-level internet traffic classifier using deep learning. In *2018 9th international conference on the network of the future (NOF)* (pp. 68–75). IEEE.

34. Lotfollahi, M., Jafari Siavoshani, M., Shirali Hossein Zade, R., & Saberian, M. (2020). Deep packet: A novel approach for encrypted traffic classification using deep learning. *Soft Computing, 24*(3), 1999–2012.

35. Shapira, T., & Shavitt, Y. (2019). Flowpic: Encrypted internet traffic classification is as easy as image recognition. In *IEEE INFOCOM 2019-IEEE conference on computer communications workshops (INFOCOM WKSHPS)* (pp. 680–687). IEEE.

36. Dong, C., Zhang, C., Lu, Z., Liu, B., & Jiang, B. (2020). CETAnalytics: Comprehensive effective traffic information analytics for encrypted traffic classification. *Computer Networks, 176*, 107258.
37. Alshammari, R., & Zincir-Heywood, A. N. (2011). Can encrypted traffic be identified without port numbers, IP addresses and payload inspection? *Computer Networks, 55*(6), 1326–1350.
38. Alshammari, R., & Zincir-Heywood, A. N. (2015). How robust can a machine learning approach be for classifying encrypted VoIP? *Journal of Network and Systems Management, 23*, 830–869.
39. Bar-Yanai, R., Langberg, M., Peleg, D., & Roditty, L. (2010). Realtime classification for encrypted traffic. In *Experimental algorithms: 9th international symposium, SEA 2010, Ischia Island, Naples, Italy, May 20–22, 2010. Proceedings 9* (pp. 373–385). Springer.
40. Zhang, M., Zhang, H., Zhang, B., & Lu, G. (2013). Encrypted traffic classification based on an improved clustering algorithm. In *Trustworthy computing and services: International conference, ISCTCS 2012, Beijing, China, May 28–June 2, 2012, Revised Selected Papers* (pp. 124–131). Springer.
41. Draper-Gil, G., Lashkari, A. H., Mamun, M. S. I., & Ghorbani, A. A. (2016). Characterization of encrypted and vpn traffic using time-related. In *Proceedings of the 2nd international conference on information systems security and privacy (ICISSP)* (pp. 407–414).
42. Gil, G. D., Lashkari, A. H., Mamun, M., & Ghorbani, A. A. (2016). Characterization of encrypted and VPN traffic using time-related features. In *Proceedings of the 2nd international conference on information systems security and privacy (ICISSP 2016)* (pp. 407–414). SciTePress.
43. Wang, D., Zhang, L., Yuan, Z., Xue, Y., & Dong, Y. (2014). February. Characterizing application behaviors for classifying p2p traffic. In *2014 international conference on computing, networking and communications (ICNC)* (pp. 21–25). IEEE.
44. Mamun, M. S. I., Ghorbani, A. A., & Stakhanova, N. (2016). An entropy based encrypted traffic classifier. In *Information and communications security: 17th international conference, ICICS 2015, Beijing, China, December 9–11, 2015, Revised Selected Papers 17* (pp. 282–294). Springer International Publishing.
45. Sherry, J., Lan, C., Popa, R. A., & Ratnasamy, S. (2015). Blindbox: Deep packet inspection over encrypted traffic. In *Proceedings of the 2015 ACM conference on special interest group on data communication* (pp. 213–226).
46. Wang, W., Shang, Y., He, Y., Li, Y., & Liu, J. (2020). BotMark: Automated botnet detection with hybrid analysis of flow-based and graph-based traffic behaviors. *Information Sciences, 511*, 284–296.
47. Cherukuri, A. K., Thaseen, I. S., Li, G., Liu, X., Das, V., & Raj, A. (2021). Integrity of IoT network flow records in encrypted traffic analytics. In *Security and privacy in the internet of things: Architectures, techniques, and applications* (pp. 177–205).
48. Wright, C., Monrose, F., & Masson, G. M. (2004). HMM profiles for network traffic classification. In *Proceedings of the 2004 ACM workshop on visualization and data mining for computer security* (pp. 9–15).
49. Hu, Y., Chiu, D. M., & Lui, J. C. (2009). Profiling and identification of P2P traffic. *Computer Networks, 53*(6), 849–863.
50. Suh, K., Figueiredo, D. R., Kurose, J., & Towsley, D. (2006). Characterizing and detecting relayed traffic: A case study using skype. *IEEE Infocom, 6.*
51. Berthier, R., Urbina, D. I., Cárdenas, A. A., Guerrero, M., Herberg, U., Jetcheva, J. G., Mashima, D., Huh, J. H., & Bobba, R. B. (2014). On the practicality of detecting anomalies with encrypted traffic in AMI. In *2014 IEEE international conference on smart grid communications (SmartGridComm)* (pp. 890–895). IEEE.
52. Anderson, B., & McGrew, D. (2016). Identifying encrypted malware traffic with contextual flow data. In *Proceedings of the 2016 ACM workshop on artificial intelligence and security* (pp. 35–46).

Chapter 4
Detection of Anomalous Encrypted Traffic

4.1   Introduction

Cryptographic protocols rely on encryption to ensure secure transmission between client and server. A wide range of cryptographic protocols namely SSL, TLS and IPSec are detailed in the introduction chapter. More specifically, SSH is a widely used protocol for authentication of clients and servers before establishing communication. All these protocols try to prevent malicious activities and eavesdropping but sometimes fail. Figure 4.1 shows an illustration of how the encrypted data is vulnerable to eavesdropping. In the first chapter, an illustration of a TLS server hello message is shown which is captured using the Wireshark tool. The packet capture clearly shows the various cipher suites used by the server. The attacker can utilise this information to eavesdrop and decrypt the data using the encryption, hashing and key exchange algorithm along with the bit size information available in the packet capture. Similarly, SSH protocol is targeted to eavesdrop the passwords. A denial-of-service (DoS) and covert channel attack are also performed on SSH traffic. Figure 4.2 shows an illustration of eavesdropping on SSH traffic. The password which is sent from A to C is eavesdropped by the adversary. A session spying is performed, and the remote host is changed by impersonation once the password is leaked. The other attacks performed on SSH are SYN flooding, TCP RST, bogus ICMP and TCP desynchronisation and hijacking. A sample representation of a bogus ICMP packet captured in the Wireshark panel is shown in Fig. 4.3. The error packets are highlighted in black or red colour in the top panel. The ICMP bogus packet is an error packet which resulted due to the eavesdropping in SSH traffic and the TTL (time-to-live) exceeded in transit. Thus, there is a need to prevent such man-in-the-middle (MITM) attacks aiming at specific protocols which is detailed in the next section.

© The Author(s), under exclusive license to Springer Nature Switzerland AG 2024   61
A. K. Cherukuri et al., *Encrypted Network Traffic Analysis*, SpringerBriefs in
Computer Science, https://doi.org/10.1007/978-3-031-62909-9_4

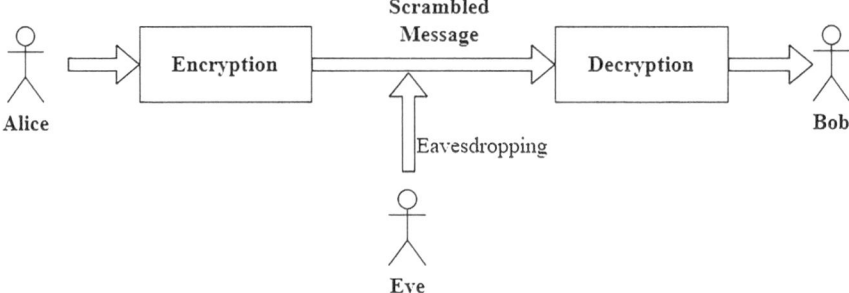

Fig. 4.1 Man-in-the-middle attack against encrypted protocols

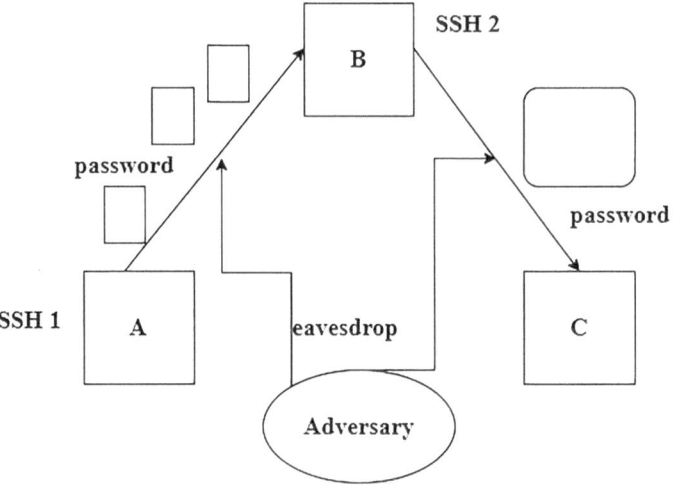

Fig. 4.2 Eavesdropping on SSH traffic

In the following sections, we discuss the detection and traceback schemes to identify the attacks against encrypted protocols by categorising them as low interactive and most interactive.

4.2   Detecting Attacks Against Encrypted Protocols

There is a significant increase in the number of attacks performed against encrypted protocols, and this is due to the uncontrolled advance of the Internet and the networks-based applications resulting in massive security leakages. Thus, it is obvious that there will be a rise in threats to encrypted protocols. Adaptive selective cipher-text attacks were hypothetically possible, especially when there was a successful threat against systems using the Public Key Cryptography Standards (PKCS)

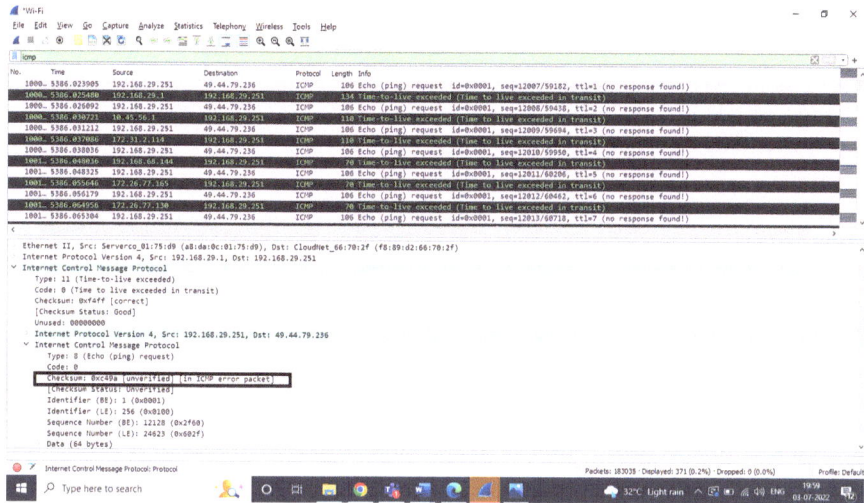

Fig. 4.3 ICMP bogus packet captured during SSH eavesdropping

encoding function integrated with RSA. These attacks targeted the encrypted web servers by transmitting trial-and-error-based cipher text with size of several millions [1]. In addition, the timing attack developed by Boneh and Brumley [2] designed an advancement in network security by mining the remote keys from an OpenSSL-based web server in a minimum of 6 h. Similar attacks against SSH such as portable open SSH PAM timing threats were also identified [3].

4.3   Tracing Back Attackers Against Encrypted Protocols

The challenge of locating attackers is an open issue over the years. Some traditional traceback approaches utilise Timed Efficient Stream Loss-Tolerant Authentication (TESLA) variant protocol to create a code, according to the router's IP address, to analyse the packets sequentially. There is a provision for every attack victim to build an IP address map so that the packet route is reconstructed for a maximum of 32 devices [4]. The challenge researchers face with regard to location tracking of the attackers is to determine the packet route with a nil increase in the packet size. There are other location-tracking approaches which result in additional packet size while sending through the routers. The origin of the routing device is determined only after the victim host has obtained the original and additional packets. This causes a surge in network traffic. Therefore, a solution is to add an additional "trace packet" on a probability basis. This technique is practical when there are many attack packets (e.g., TCP SYN-flood) which are long-lasting, e.g. for every 20,000 packets, there will be one new trace packet.

Probabilistic packet marking (PPM) [5] and its improved variant [6] are few traceback approaches, and other packet marking techniques [7] require the IP header information. Therefore, the location of the traceback of the attacker sending encrypted packets is difficult since decryption of the attack packet headers have to be computed by the traceback modules.

4.4   Detection and Traceback Schemes

A Detection and Traceback Scheme (DTRAB) is developed [8] as traditional approaches do not succeed to handle these threats.

4.4.1   Envisioned Attacks

The various attack categories which DTRAB will address are discussed in this section. For example, the OpenSSL implementation is vulnerable to man-in-the-middle (MITM), remote timing, version pushback and buffer overflow. In case of password attack and SSL negotiation attack (also called as the brute force or dictionary attack) against SSH which are remote timing attacks, highest association is present among the cryptographic protocol server and the attacker. In addition, scanning attacks analyse the presence and configuration of a basic HTTP web/proxy server which can also result in a major volume of attack attributes. Similar characteristics are also exhibited for directory-traversal attacks which are broadly called "most interactive attacks". On the conflicting note in buffer overflow, only minimal communications are sent between the client and server. Arbitrary code is executed on the server victim resulting in an overwriting of process heap or stack memory. These attacks are named as "low interactive attacks". Also, the cross-scripting results in attack vulnerabilities are termed as "low interactive attacks".

4.4.2   Network Topology

In this section a scenario which is shown in Fig. 4.4 is described as follows. An IDS is designed uniquely by envisioning techniques, which are named as monitoring stubs (MSs). The proposed MSs are dispersed (e.g., edge routers, gateways and few core routers) [8] on the entire network. Figure 4.4 consists of multiple servers executing various services on application-based and encrypted protocols. Internet users on untrusted networks can associate to such servers. Nearly seven MSs are located on the network sideways. The MSs do not analyse the payload. When the host initiates an attack (in Network-1), in an insecure network to the victim server, MS can consecutively analyse invasion as an attack attribute. In addition, the regular

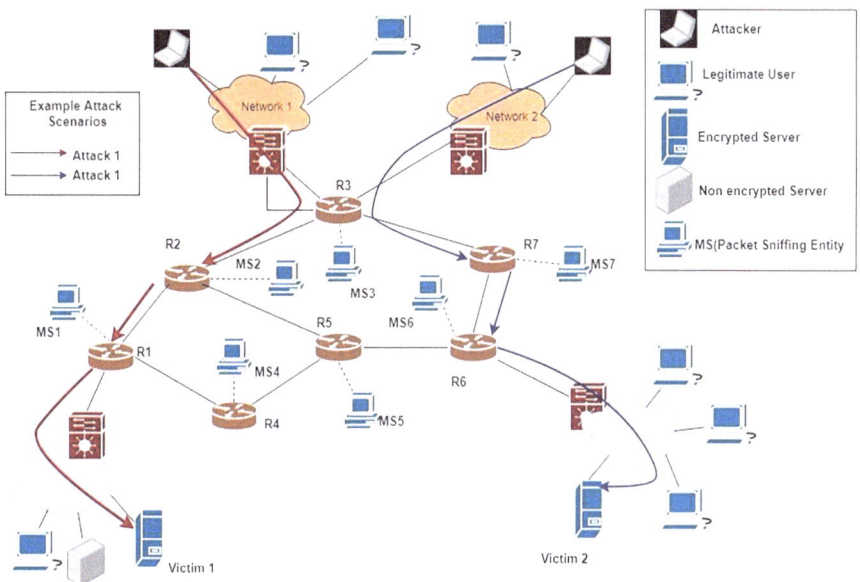

Fig. 4.4 Example scenario for attack illustration [8]

operation and request-for-comments (RFCs) of diverse protocols in the MS records can be extended to identify threats against regular application-level data.

The network traffic is slowed down as an MS is only sniffing packets situated on the side of a router. It is an insignificant operation to sniff and analyse the packet headers and the payload for the application-level protocols. A different approach has to be adopted by MS for encrypted protocols. The TCP headers of unencrypted protocols are monitored by the TCPDUMP tool which is utilised by the MS. For instance, to identify an unsuccessful SSH session because of a password attack on port 22, MS needs to investigate the SSH protocol in the transport layer. Figure 4.5 shows the initial stage wherein the client sends an SYN packet to connect to the server. An ACK and a SYN packet is sent as a response by the server. Once the client has successfully logged on to the server and wishes to leave, the finish flag (FIN) packets are sent by the client. In case, the server wishes to close the connection due to an error attempt to avail the service or a timeout, the server sends the FIN packets first. An MS observes the flows in a connection, and if the server has sent the FIN packet initially, it observes a deviation and assumes that as a "failed session". An MS investigates abnormal protocol behaviour when the encrypted web traffic flow is analysed using SSL/TLS. The analysis will consider request size proportion to the equivalent response size. The short interactive attacks launched on encrypted web servers utilise HTTPS services, and MS can retrieve such attack data. In case of non-encrypted traffic, this can be easily determined by observing the packet information. However, as the headers are encrypted in HTTPS, it is tough to extract the request and response size. In addition, the SSL packets are padded with 255 bytes

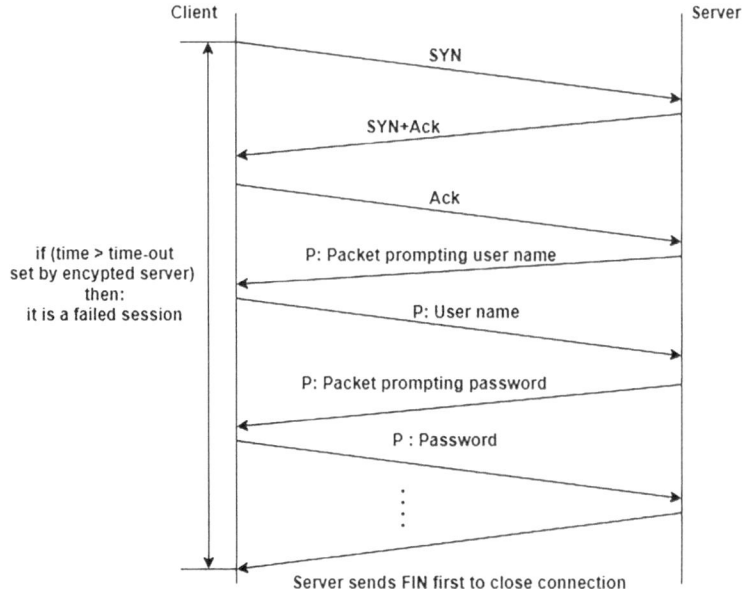

Fig. 4.5 SSH Connection-flow-based failed session design

of random data. The client requests are checked by MS on port 443. If there is continuous flow of packets, it can be assumed as an individual operation, such as a link click or request to download a file. The headers of TCP sessions are reconstructed by the MS during the evaluation. The request and response size is determined by the MS after decoding the SSL/TLS session from the server.

This is because the header fragment of the "record layer" in an SSL/TLS packet is encrypted whereas the other three headers, such as "length", "type" and "version" remain unencrypted. It is observed that such attack attributes are not manually picked; instead every MS maintains an archive of RFCs conditions for the utilisation of multiple encrypted and unencrypted protocols. The MS analyses the normal profile, monitors for abnormalities deviating from the normal behaviour, alerts generation and locates the attacker. The functioning approaches of an MS are given below:

4.4.3 DTRAB Learning Stage

It is important to study the protocol implementations and RFCs which are standard documents to precisely identify anomalous behaviours, from which it is possible to explain the normal protocol mode of operation. In addition, the protocol behaviour varies in different intervals. For example, a corporate website will be browsed heavily throughout the day, and minimal at night. The effect of these aspects can be shown as a statistical profile over time built during the normal network activities of the learning phase with minimal level of illegitimate actions. Every MS in the envisioned network has a database containing the unencrypted header features of the periodically monitored traffic.

The MS analyses various protocol actions to identify the attacks. The observed values serve as input to the CUSUM nonparametric technique which is utilised by the MSs in the identification phase. The primary fields such as total unsuccessful sessions and complete sessions represented by S_n and T_n are sampled over the profiling time. The results are used to compute the segment of the failed session and then stored in the database.

4.4.4   DTRAB Detection Stage

This approach is mainly used for identifying anomalies. This phase focuses on the quick change in the behaviour of the encrypted protocol to detect the attack. A statistical tool namely the Cusum technique is utilised. The classical Cusum technique is expensive due to the demanding nature to analyse the statistical probabilities of legitimate and anomalous event hypotheses. However, it is not possible to model the Internet traffic according to this hypothesis. Hence, the nonparametric type of Cusum is incorporated which is lightweight and suitable to the scope of encrypted traffic. This scheme is also useful because the knowledge of traffic distribution was not required previously. As the MSs are deployed with the Cusum algorithm, the MSs can identify the point of changes in the network when an anomaly occurs. This advantage of identifying the minimal variations in the network profile, and the simplicity at which they are constructed in the MS emboldens the use of this technique in the tool.

This approach is analysed with an example of random arrangement wherein the sum of unsuccessful SSH connections in a network flow is considered over an interval. The failed session ratio F_n is determined over a time limit. Let "m" represent the mean of F_n over the profiling interval of normal situation. The value of "m" is under 1 and is closer to zero until the system observes an anomaly for legitimate SSH traffic. Therefore, F_n is modelled as a static stochastic method and the mean variation of F_n is determined using the Cusum approach. The random sequence mean is assumed as negative for normal situations and converts to positive if there is a change. Thus F_n is transformed into a new sequence G_n. The online attack problem identification is resolved by utilising a nonparametric Cusum technique which is represented by a novel sequence Y_n. A Y_n with greater value represents the abnormal behaviour, i.e., an attack. If there is no attack, G_n values lie typically less bounded. During an attack, the G_n becomes positive and is very large. At the identification stage, Y_n is determined by MS. The value will stay closer to zero. The MSs in the DTRAB approach observe the early handshakes present in the flows. This process initiates the cryptographic connections and retrieves the required attributes (e.g., failed sessions). Hence, all state information of every connection is not analysed by MS in individual flows, which would have caused scalability problems.

4.4.5   DTRAB Alert Stage

When an anomaly is identified by the nonparametric Cusum approach, there is an increase in the Y_n sequence. Once Y_n surpasses zero, an alert is generated by the MSs to the neighbouring MSs and the server. The MS requests the server to minimise the protocol response to stop anomalies such as remote timing threats.

4.4.6   DTRAB Traceback Phase

In this phase, the mechanism proceeds with the association of the MSs to analyse abnormal protocol operations (e.g., unsuccessful session rates) over a period. Each and every MS stores the failed session information in the database which it monitors for internal and external traffic. The records comprise a list of associating MSs, with which the MS can communicate such that the attack path is reconstructed. If the attack is detected, the victim encrypted server nearest to the MS server enters into the "Traceback mode".

4.5   Performance Analysis

The DTRAB performance is evaluated with light scale simulations and computer network experiments. The DTRAB detection approach is applied on various unencrypted Internet traces of CAIDA datasets [9].

4.5.1   Highly Collaborative Attack Detection

Each MS sniffs and monitors the encrypted traffic. Therefore, detection performance at every single MS is not required. The MSs which are located single hop far from the cryptographic server are analysed for assessing the identification approach. An SSH server is targeted and a customised SSH traffic originator is built at the client side, running on Windows XP SSH-2 protocol. The sniffer runs on a server which acts as a monitoring stub configured as virtual machine (VM).The SSH connection arrivals in the normal scenario follow a Gamma distribution. It is possible that a few users can enter the authentication information incorrectly which can result in attack-like attributes to be inserted into the network traffic. It is however very minimal in normal profile.

4.5.2   Detection Accuracy

Multiple password attacks with various aggressive levels targeting the SSH protocol are launched against the server to determine the detection sensitivity of DTRAB. A new metric called "failed session detection error rate" is calculated as the number of unnoticed failed connections to the total number of unsuccessful sessions. This metric surges when the approach is identifying attacks with minimal attack aggressive level. The parameter Y_n can be reset to zero when the first attack is detected by MS. In certain cases if the attack continues, the Y_n will rise, thereby exceeding the threshold in the next interval. As a result, more alerts will be generated for the same identified attack. This issue is solved by creating a cluster of Cusum objects. Once an abnormality is identified, a new profile is created by the MS removing the doubtful clients. The MS monitors the distribution of the Cusum approach continuously to check if the attack recedes with respect to the initial profile. In addition, the next monitoring method remains to execute utilising the latest created profile. When the MS identifies an attack in the second Cusum distribution entity, then another profile will be created by the MS. Thus, the traceback parameter is determined based on how long the observed failed session rates collaborate with the monitoring ends. The nonparametric Cusum technique utilised minimal memory for the experiment. In case of simultaneous attacks, every entity of the identification phase consumed nearly 5588–5592 KB memory for code execution. The CPU utilisation was only 50% with four entities of the identification process executing continuously.

CAIDA datasets are applied on the DTRAB detection approach due to the difficulty in obtaining the real encrypted web-based network traffic. The dataset consists of raw traffic of 9 years starting from 2001 till 2009. In the initial experiments, Backscatter-2008 CAIDA dataset is utilised, which consist of spoofed traffic responses captured in a quarterly week-long collection. A spoofed source IP address is received by the DoS attack victim. As it is not possible to differentiate between the legitimate and spoofed request, the spoofed source receives the response (second phase of the TCP handshake) and an ACK message is sent to finish the TCP handshake. The DTRAB scheme analyses the incomplete session information from the dataset which in maximum consists of legitimate traffic and few attack traces. This detection approach is also applied on Witty worms and Code Red II worms of the CAIDA datasets. The MSs in the networks execute the Cusum approach to identify the abnormal protocol behaviour. One such anomaly is observed based on the rate of outgoing sessions a particular host wishes to start in a given interval. A high detection latency is observed in a particular monitoring interval because the worm is dormant up to a certain time. However, when the worm is active, DTRAB identifies the anomalous rise in the number of outgoing sessions in the network. Therefore, infections to other hosts are prohibited by warning the corresponding network admin/server.

4.6   Traceback Scheme Performance

The performance is estimated with two simulation scenarios. In the first case, simultaneous threats are initiated against two victim servers located in two diverse networks. Simulations are run for five times. In the next scenario, the convergence points of DTRAB's traceback approach is analysed and related with the traditional approach [10].

4.6.1   Tracing Back Multiple Attackers

The performance of the approach is determined by launching simultaneous attacks from diverse sources to more than one target. The topology consists of seven MSs which are constructed using NS-2. The scalability of DTRAB can be determined by the approach in which the MSs collaborate with one another to accomplish traceback. It is to be noted that even with few MSs, the MSs work collaboratively in their neighbour zone which assists in correlating traffic with MSs which are very far and can still locate the path. Attacks targeting the password based on SSH originating from two malicious users in two diverse networks N_1 and N_2 are replicated against two target cryptographic servers. The correlation coefficients for various pairs of flows are investigated. Three such pairings are identified: normal versus normal, malicious versus malicious and malicious versus normal flows. Let c_1 specify the correlation coefficient (between MS_1 and MS_2) and c_2 specify the correlation coefficient (between MS_2 and MS_3) of vectors containing malicious features. Let c_3 specify the correlation coefficient (between MS_1 and MS_4) and c_4 specify the correlation coefficient (between MS_2 and MS_5) and c_5 specify the correlation coefficient (between MS_3 and MS_7) of the vectors, respective flows consisting of attributes which are normal in one and attack attributes in the other. Let c_6 (between MS_4 and MS_5), c_7 (between MS_5 and MS_6) and c_8 (between MS_6 and MS_7) characterise the vector correlation coefficient of normal flows.

   The results indicate that c_1 and c_2 have high correlation for different attack aggressiveness. However, c_3, c_4 and c_5 represent correlation values near to zero for diverse attack aggressiveness. If the attack aggressive is high, c_3, c_4 and c_5 result in negative value. The results are approved with the traceback decision along the actual way. An important point to be noted is that c_6, c_7 and c_8 have high correlation values and remain the same with various attack aggressive levels. The reason is the attack traffic was not diverse through the respective MSs. This condition on every subsequent MSs had nil effect on the traceback operation and therefore no possibility for comparisons.

4.6.2   Investigating the Convergence Point Influence

In this case, the applicability of DTRAB under the confluence point influence is verified [11]. When a DDoS attack is initiated from multiple sources, the traditional method of comparing correlated traffic patterns at various points in the network is not satisfactory. The DTRAB mechanism addresses this problem by assuming quadratic programming wherein the combination of DDoS input traffic is also considered. Hence, real Internet traffic traces are congregated from the Tohoku University Aobayama campus, Japan, and the quadratic approach is adopted. Thus, in this approach, DTRAB can differentiate traffic of single attack flows with 100% success ratio. The superior performance of DTRAB is due to the fact that the comparison is based on non-attack flows, which are monitored and contribute to minimal attack attributes. The traceback decision of DTRAB increases linearly with increasing number of flows. For example, it takes approximately 15 ms for DTRAB to identify the real attack path, however it takes almost 60 ms to discover attack flows. It should also be noted that if the number of attack flows at the convergence exceeds six, the computation time of the traditional approach also increases suggestively. Thus, the trade-off between the DTRAB's success rate and computation time is still satisfactory.

4.7   Conclusion

In this chapter, we have discussed the various attacks that are targeted against encrypted protocols such as TLS and SSH and their defence mechanisms in detail. Two different cases for tracing and identifying the attackers are investigated by developing defence strategies and their performance is evaluated. In the next chapter, we will discuss machine learning and deep learning approaches for encrypted traffic classification in detail.

References

1. Fadlullah, Z. M., Taleb, T., Ansari, N., Hashimoto, K., Miyake, Y., Nemoto, Y., & Kato, N. (2007). Combating against attacks on encrypted protocols. In *2007 IEEE international conference on communications* (pp. 1211–1216). IEEE.
2. Wang, H., Zhang, D., & Shin, K. G. (2004). Change-point monitoring for the detection of DoS attacks. *IEEE Transactions on Dependable and Secure Computing, 1*(4), 193–208.
3. Anderson, J. P. (1980). *Computer security threat monitoring and surveillance* (Technical Report). James P. Anderson Company.
4. Park, K., & Lee, H. (2001). On the effectiveness of probabilistic packet marking for IP traceback under denial of service attack. In *Proceedings IEEE INFOCOM 2001. Conference on computer communications. Twentieth annual joint conference of the IEEE computer and communications society (Cat. No. 01CH37213)*, vol. 1 (pp. 338–347). IEEE.

5. Belenky, A., & Ansari, N. (2003). On IP traceback. *IEEE Communications Magazine, 41*(7), 142–153.
6. Law, T. K. T., Lui, J. C. S., & Yau, D. K. Y. (2005). You can run, but you can't hide: An effective statistical methodology to trace back DDoS attackers. *IEEE Transactions on Parallel and Distributed Systems, 16*(9), 799–813.
7. Gao, Z., & Ansari, N. (2005). Tracing cyber attacks from the practical perspective. *IEEE Communications Magazine, 43*(5), 123–131.
8. Fadlullah, Z. M., Taleb, T., Vasilakos, A. V., Guizani, M., & Kato, N. (2010). DTRAB: Combating against attacks on encrypted protocols through traffic-feature analysis. *IEEE/ACM Transactions on Networking, 18*(4), 1234–1247.
9. "CAIDA: The Cooperative Association for Internet Data Analysis," [Online]. Available: http://www.caida.org/home/
10. Mansfield, G., Ohta, K., Takei, Y., Kato, N., & Nemoto, Y. (2000). Towards trapping wily intruders in the large. *Computer Networks, 34*(4), 659–670.
11. Sakaguchi, K., Ohta, K., Waizumi, Y., Kato, N., & Nemoto, Y. (2002). Tracing DDoS attacks by comparing traffic patterns based on quadratic programming methods. *Transactions IEICE B, 85*(8), 1295–1303.

Chapter 5
Artificial Intelligence-Based Approaches for Anomaly Detection

5.1 Introduction

There is an enormous increase in the generation of encrypted traffic volume, as there is a demand for privacy and data security. The increasing trend of encrypted traffic from the past 7 years (2014 to 2021) is analysed in the Google report [1]. There is a sharp increase in the Internet encrypted traffic from 50% to 95% in the past 7 years. Another report generated by Desai [2] observed that there are more than 500% upsurges in ransomware and 260% rise in Secure Sockets Layer (SSL)-centred attacks. In addition, the report also inferred that the existing cybersecurity mechanisms do not analyse the complete network traffic. Traffic classification is severely challenged by both the evolving traffic nature traversing the current networks and volume. This also impacts the ways users interact and access the network. The difficulty of traffic classification increases, due to the widespread acceptance of encrypted protocols such as Transport Layer Security and also the use of network address translation. Tor and IPSec technologies can shield listeners' communication data, resulting in anonymous senders. The payload is inaccessible for third parties. However, information can be obtained based on the size and timing of individual packets. The encrypted data is pseudorandom in nature. The process of dividing and recombining the network payload will clearly represent this statistical law, thereby assisting ML or DL models to accelerate the statistical attribute learning [3]. In this chapter, various machine learning and deep learning approaches utilised for classifying encrypted traffic are discussed in detail. The performance of various ML algorithms and the impact of various attributes of different types of ML models is analysed. A summary of DL models used for encrypted traffic classification is also detailed.

The rest of the chapter is organised as follows: Section 5.1 discusses traffic classification using traditional techniques. Sections 5.2 and 5.3 detail ML- and DL-based approaches for encrypted traffic classification. Section 5.5 presents the proposed models developed for encrypted traffic classification.

5.2 Machine Learning-Based Approaches for Encrypted Traffic Analysis

The traditional approach to network traffic categorisation is to analyse the payload of every packet. This technique can be tremendously accurate when the payload is unencrypted. However, encrypted applications such as SSH (Secure Shell), VPN, IPSec, Skype and Tor infer that the payload is dense. Another approach to classify applications is by using TCP/UDP port numbers. This approach is inaccurate when applications utilise non-standard ports to evade firewalls or avoid operating system restrictions. Thus, other sophisticated techniques are required to categorise encrypted traffic with increase in accuracy. Recent research in this area concentrates on the classification of efficient and effective classifiers. Various research groups have employed diverse machine learning approaches such as hidden Markov models (HMM), Naïve Bayesian models, AdaBoost or maximum entropy. These sophisticated approaches have proven to be superior to the traditional methods as they do not require any payload, IP addresses or port numbers [4]. These algorithms enhance the accuracy and efficiency of encrypted malicious traffic identification.

Machine learning models require an important and sufficient learning number of samples to identify the behaviours [5]. These models can determine complex patterns with many attributes. ML-based cybersecurity techniques have made promising contributions in identifying various types of attacks, such as distributed denial-of-service (DDoS), Portscan, bot and web attacks.

5.2.1 Attribute-Based Analysis

Traffic classifications at the flow level for ML-based approaches are primarily based on compound manual attributes based on experts' opinion. Figure 5.1 shows the traffic classification using machine learning approaches. In the first stage, flow-based features are extracted and then sent to a machine learning classifier to predict the output label. Moore et al. [6] built a model with about 250 attributes based on prior information. In addition, the other traffic classification literature [5, 7, 8] are

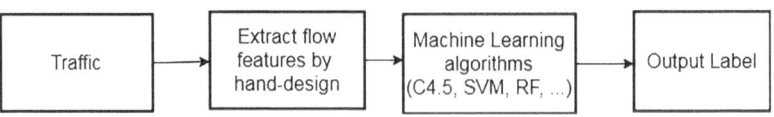

Fig. 5.1 Traffic classification using machine learning approaches

also based on these 250 features for attribute extraction. These flow attributes include packet byte variances, total bytes in IP packets and median of the packets. The other attributes also to be analysed are as follows:

5.2.1.1 Packet Size and Inter-Arrival Time (IAT)

Two of the most direct attributes extracted from the encrypted network traffic streams are packet size and inter-arrival time. The payload is directly proportional to the packet size, which is based on the explicit criteria used for application categorisation. A symbol indicates the packet direction, a negative sign represents response traffic and a positive symbol represents request traffic.

The packet size has a constraint because of the privacy-preserving protocols that compress the payload encrypted with a pseudorandom byte value or by converting to same-sized packets. The flexibility of inter-arrival time is minimal. It is therefore suggested to combine both features and obtain a derived attribute.

5.2.1.2 Burst Size-Surge Duration

A burst is described as the order of the non-acknowledgement packets sent between the incoming and outgoing direction. The surge period is used along with the burst size.

Fu et al. [9] used HMM to integrate user and network behaviour for categorising the mobile messaging services. Yao et al. [10] categorised the complicated traffic with HMM and Gaussian mixture models to enhance the flow attribute accuracy by determining the relation between packet size and internal packet arrival time. Thus, these classifiers can analyse most of the flow packets or entire flow packets for offline traffic identification. Machine learning (ML) classifiers have also been adapted to encrypted traffic (ET), and they are best suited for modern traffic classification without requiring port or address information [11]. There have been great results on feature engineering using machine learning approaches such as SVM and RF [12]. In this technique, features are extracted manually by applying expert knowledge. Three machine learning models were identified, and the best is chosen for monitoring the encrypted traffic exchanged between clients and servers [13]. The model was trained on 70 ransomware binaries from 26 different strains. The results show that the proposed work can identify the binaries which were not present in the training phase. A time-based filtering and parameter tuning is deployed for machine learning. Three models were chosen: DT, three ensembles (TEs) and neural networks (NN). It is observed that NN achieves more than 99% result for all the metrics.

Small and fast-to-execute machine learning approaches analyse the attributes retrieved from ET which are used for identifying the traffic passing through Tor channel or IPSec [14]. This model improves the network quality-of-service (QoS) in real time. Tor preserves anonymity by building a relay node network which is more complex in comparison to IPSec. Tables 5.1 and 5.2 present the IPSec and Tor encrypted data results [14]. In Tables 5.1 and 5.2, it is shown that the classifier results in a better score for IPSec and Tor traffic if the features are integrated rather than individual in nature. It is evident that there is the highest accuracy of 96.77% obtained by Random Forest for the integrated features of IPSec traffic. Similarly, the highest accuracy of 83% is obtained for Tor traffic by Naïve Bayes, which is a good score.

Zhu and Zheng [15] analysed the network traffic by using the TCP flags and packet size to convert the given problem into high-dimensional attribute space using a kernel function. SVM classifier was used for prediction. A three-layer IDS uses a supervised technique [16] to identify popular cyberattacks on IoT networks. This model is tested by executing 12 network attacks under 4 main categories namely DoS, Replay, Spoofing and Reconnaissance. In addition, the model is also evaluated against four use cases of multi-stage attacks containing complex events. A higher performance is obtained for F-measure on three core functions resulting in 96.2, 90.0 and 98.0%.

Binary identification of SSH versus non-SSH traffic is implemented using various machine learning approaches, namely C4.5 and multi-objective genetic algorithm (MOGA) [17]. It was observed that MOGA minimised the complexity of the model and C4.5 produced quick results.

Canavase et al. [18] identified the tools which can generate encrypted traffic using machine learning approaches. The classification is done by analysing the TCP connection flow statistics. Thus, it is likely to classify HTTP and HTTPS traffic, as the results are not dependent on the transport layer payload. The primary aim of this classification is to identify DDoS attacks early. Another aim is to avoid web forgery and starvation of site resources. The various models trained to perform the classification are RF, extra-trees and a neural network (NN). The best accuracy, F-score and classification time of 94%, 89% and 2.54 microseconds, respectively, are achieved in the RF model for identifying the tool category. Similarly, RF performs better in accuracy and F-score for classifying the tool instance but the classification time is huge because of the difficulty in classification. A limitation of this work is that they cannot handle UDP traffic. An ensemble learning-based RF classifier is deployed to analyse Domain Name System (DNS) over HTTPS (DoH) dataset (CIRA-CIC-DoHBrW-2020) with 30 features [19]. The proposed model resulted in 100% accuracy. DoH requests and responses are encrypted and require HTTP or HTTP/2 protocols instead of UDP. The proposed ML-based automation model is used to identify if the DoH traffic is vulnerable or compromised. Machine learning

Table 5.1 Analysing accuracy of various feature spaces for various machine learning approaches on IPSec encrypted data

Feature	Naïve Bayes (NB) (%)	Logistic Regression (LR) (%)	Random Forest (RF) (%)
Size-IAT	93.55	95.70	96.77
Burst	87.10	94.62	93.55
Integrated	94.62	95.70	96.77

Table 5.2 Analysing accuracy of various feature spaces for various machine learning approaches on Tor encrypted data

Feature	Naïve Bayes (%)	Logistic regression (%)	Random forest (%)
Size-IAT	80.56	77.78	84.72
Burst	86.11	80.56	86.11
Integrated	83.33	80.56	80.56

approaches assist to recognise behaviours of encrypted protocols. The generalisation issue encountered by the classical classifiers might be solved by the integration of several classifiers. The performance is improved by specialised classifiers. The major issue in most of the ML solutions is that when new patterns are identified in the network, the ML models must be updated. ML-based classification is pruned to be out-of-date quickly, due to the network dynamism. Hence, self-learning, evolving or retraining approaches must be considered. In most of the ML approaches, an update means the model has to be retrained with a new labelled dataset [20]. Hence, the model has to be retrained continuously whenever a new behaviour or application is identified in the network. This factor is very important to be considered, otherwise there will be a risk in model performance. Therefore, the encrypted traffic classification is extended to deep learning models because of the following reasons: DL models do not require significant human effort, and they are not reliant on the feature choice. DL models can build various representative layers and effective algorithms to retrieve hidden knowledge from massive amounts of traffic data deprived of feature engineering.

DL models (e.g. LSTM) are proficient in handling temporal-spatial data, and analysing related dependencies. Most network management information collected as time-series datasets can be analysed by DL models with high accuracy [21].

5.3   Deep Learning-Based Approaches for Encrypted Traffic Analysis

When applying ML techniques to examine network traffic, it can be divided into two types: shallow and deep learning. The prediction accuracy of encrypted network traffic is not very high in traditional techniques [22].

There has been incredible development in many applications using deep learning approaches [23]. Image classification [24] is widely done using Convolutional Neural Networks (CNNs). In addition, they are implemented in various fields [24] namely, sentence classification, medical imaging, genomics, age and gender identification.

Deep learning models can be broadly categorised into three classes, which are unsupervised, supervised and hybrid mechanisms. The various models under each category [25] are represented in Fig. 5.2.

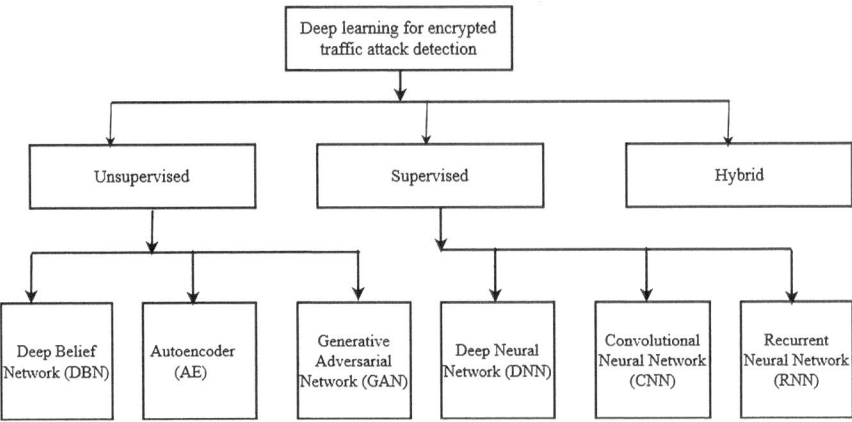

Fig. 5.2 Current deep learning approaches used for encrypted traffic detection

Table 5.3 Summary of the deep learning-based traffic classification approaches

DL models	Model input	Dataset	Classification task	Granularity
MLP,SAE [27]	Raw packet	Private	Traffic classification	Application
MLP,SAE, CNN [28]	Raw packet	ISCX 2012	Encrypted traffic classification	Application
MLP,SAE, CNN [2]	Raw packet	ISCX 2012	Encrypted traffic classification	Application
CNN [29]	Raw data	USTC-TFC2016	Malware classification	Application
CNN [30]	Raw data	ISCX 2012	–	Encrypted traffic classification
CNN, LSTM [8]	Packet-level features	Private dataset	Traffic classification	Application
MLP,SAE, CNN,LSTM [31]	Raw data	Private dataset	Mobile traffic classification	Application
CNN,RF [32]	Packet-level features	Private dataset	QUIC encrypted traffic	Application
GAN (generative adversarial networks)	Raw data	National Institute of Material Sciences (NIMS)	Encrypted traffic classification	Protocol
CNN [33]	Raw data	Private dataset	Traffic classification	Protocol/application

A deep learning model has to be trained to build a representative, huge and balanced dataset [26]. The process of selecting data, collecting data and generating samples are performed using different techniques given below. A summary of few recent works for traffic classification using DL approaches is detailed in Table 5.3.

5.3.1 Data Preprocessing

In some of the works, raw data is collected from ISP's network or research lab to build their own dataset like USTC-TFC2016 and IMTD17. Most of the literature works selected 70 K–1500 K samples for training, in which most of them are encrypted traffic records. In addition, most of the literature chose 5–17 applications or protocols for their classification. Therefore, there is no publicly available dataset due to the following causes: (1) no dataset can have all types of application traffic due to the large numbers of traffic categories and application updates frequency; (2) it is very costly, time-consuming and hard to analyse all the network scenarios like radio access and broadband services. Thus, it is impossible to create a dataset that can precisely and comprehensively characterise the traffic distribution. It is observed from Table 5.3, the authors [8, 27, 33] collected raw data from ISP's network. Raw packets are collected by Tcpdump tool [34] and other workflow tools like NetFlow [35] are used to gather traffic records. Data expansion is performed to create new samples to balance the majority and minority classes. Undersampling and oversampling techniques can be deployed to achieve the balance in the dataset. The dataset traffic is divided into raw packet samples, PCAP records and statistical attributes. Data in the first two categories has to be preprocessed for the following reasons: (1) there are some unrelated packets, such as ARP, DHCP and ICMP in raw packet samples; (2) attribute distribution at the packet level may be biased by few unpredicted situations in the network such as out of order and retransmission packets; (3) PCAP header is irrelevant information in PCAP files. Hence, packet filtering and header removal are essential [28, 30]. Fixed-size truncation and zero-padding are required for raw data in most cases. This is because deep neural network (DNN) requires an input of fixed size, whereas the packet frame length in the dataset can vary between 54 to 1514 bytes for the TCP. Data normalisation is vital for the deep learning performance to increase. Thus, the convergence is quicker during the model training phase (Table 5.4).

5.3.2 Traffic Attributes

The traffic classification input to a DL model can be classified into three types: raw packet data, traffic attributes and combination with raw data and attributes. The summary of model input existing in the literature is shown in Table 5.5. In most of the existing works, raw packets are chosen as the input to the model [27, 29]. As mentioned in section B, truncation and zero-padding are mandatory. It is observed from Table 5.5 that zero-padding and truncation size can vary between 700 and 1500 bytes. The more first packets are analysed, the more flow attributes are comprehensively studied. This factor has a huge impact on classifier performance. In [9], packet-level attributes such as source and destination port, TCP window size, packet direction and inter-arrival time are analysed. In [32], a combination of raw

Table 5.4 Summary of datasets used in the existing works

Work	Dataset	Samples	Application numbers	Encrypted	Balanced
Wang [27]	Private	300 K	58	Yes	N/A
Datanet [2]	ISCX 2012	73 K	15	Yes	Yes
Deep packet [28]	ISCX2012	22,293 K	17	Yes	Yes
2D-CNN [29]	USTC-TFC2016	752 K	20	Yes	Yes
1D-CNN [30]	ISCX2012	N/A	12	Yes	N/A
Lopez-Martin [8]	Private	266 K	15	Yes	N/A
Aceto [31]	Private	77.5 K	49	Yes	N/A
Van [32]	Private	20 K	5	Yes	Yes
Seq2Img [33]	Private	22 K-pro/282 K-app	5-pro/5-app	Yes	Yes

Table 5.5 Summary of model input in the literature

Data type	Zero-padding length	Attributes	First packets
Raw data [27]	1000	–	–
Raw data [28]	1480	–	–
Raw data [29]	1500	–	–
Raw data [30]	784	–	–
Attributes [8]	–	Port, payload bytes, TCP window size, inter-arrival time, direction	20
Attributes [33]	–	Raw attributes—28, statistical attributes—10	10
Raw data and attributes [32]	1400	Percentage of small, medium, large packets avg. payload length	10

packet data and attributes are extracted from NetFlow to identify the Google applications using QUIC (Quick UDP Internet Connections), which is a novel encryption protocol.

5.3.3   Models

DL requires a large amount of labelled data during training but collecting a large dataset is very time-consuming and costly. However, unlabelled traffic data is available readily. DPI cannot handle traffic data like encrypted traffic. Therefore, researchers explore how to integrate easily available unlabelled traffic samples with few labelled traffic samples for efficiently classifying traffic. This resulted in a new learning called semi-supervised learning, by which one can pre-train a model D_u with large unlabelled traffic records and then assign to a novel design and relearn the model using D_l. The critical factor for traffic classification is the model architecture. A review of various model architecture designs of existing literature is given below.

5.3.3.1   MLP

Wang et al. [27] developed an MLP model for traffic classification. There were 58 protocol categories present in 0.3 million traffic samples collected from their internal network. Regular and encrypted traffic samples were present in the dataset. The experimental results show that both precision and recall achieved more than 90% on the 25 top protocols. Draper-Gill et al. [36] utilised the VPN/non-VPN traffic dataset of ISCX2012, consisting of 15 encrypted applications and 73,392 packets. MLP model is used in this analysis also. The experimental results show that precision, recall and F1-score were greater than 92%.

5.3.3.2   CNN

MLP cannot analyse high dimensional input, because there are a large number of model parameters in hidden layers. CNN improves this constraint by building a CNN with kernel set and parameters. In [29], Wang et al. used 2D-CNN for malware classification with bidirectional flow packet bytes, resulting in maximum accuracy. In addition, the same authors proposed a 1D-CNN architecture to categorise the traffic from the ISCX2012 dataset and resulted in a substantial improvement over C4.5 of ML techniques and a slight increase over 2D-CNN, which they proposed previously.

5.3.3.3   SAE

Stacked autoencoder (SAE) models proposed for traffic classification are integrated with softmax and all experimental results have proved a very outstanding performance compared to classical ML models. Such models can reduce the data dimension and rebuild the input accurately. The node numbers of the latent layer are described in Datanet [2] and deep packet [28] as 32 and 50, respectively.

5.3.3.4   VAE

Variational autoencoder can minimise the parameter constraints and enhance the error tolerating capacity of input data. In [37], the authors determined traffic through a two-stage learning, which comprised unsupervised feature selection and supervised class mapping. In the first phase, VAE selects latent attributes from heavy unlabelled samples and maps the attributes to certain classes with minimal labelled samples. A good performance is observed in the experimental results.

5.3.3.5   Denoising Auto Encoder (DAE)

A severe concern of AE is that there are more nodes in the hidden layer than the input layer. AEs are risking to make the output equal to input to learn the identity function also known as the null function, thereby rendering the AEs useless. DAE solves this problem by randomly changing a few input values to zero. The loss function is calculated by comparing the output results with the original value, not with the random value. Thus, the learning risk of the identity function is removed. Some existing works utilised DAE for IDS and Network Anomaly Identification [38, 39].

5.3.3.6   GAN

An optimal solution at convergence [40] is obtained using the two networks in GAN, the generator and discriminator network, in order to produce. In [41], the authors synthesised traffic using AC-GAN (unsupervised auxiliary classifier) to balance the major and minor classes on a reputed dataset known as NIMS which contained only two classes namely SSH and non-SSH. This model analysed both class label and noise as input to determine the sample input class label. The proposed approach resulted in a good performance compared to SMOTE (Synthetic Minority Over-Sampling Technique). Thus, GAN is mainly used in IDS and malware identification [42].

Deep learning (DL) approaches have been widely used in traffic classification. Liu et al. [43] derived the forward and backward attributes of the flow byte sequence using a bidirectional gated recurrent unit (Bi-GRU). Liu et al. [44] obtained the hidden information in the packet length sequence using Bi-GRU. A novel technique [45] named MATEC (maximizing the reuse of thin modules) to derive high order flow-based attributes is proposed. A multi-head attention mechanism allows each packet to communicate with all other packets for ET classification. Experimental analysis proves that the ET precision is enhanced by 1.7%.

Deep packet [28] for traffic flow categorisation is based on the DL approach that combines both attribute removal and prediction into one model. In this approach, encrypted traffic detects end-user applications (e.g. Skype). In this technique, the encrypted traffic across VPN (Virtual Private Network) is identified using two DL classifiers: Stacked autoencoder (SAE) and CNN. The CNN model results in a classification rate of 94%. Deep-Full-Range (DFR) was developed [46] to identify encrypted network traffic. The various models used in this approach are Long Short-Term Memory (LSTM), CNN and SAE. A comparative analysis using two public datasets is performed with contemporary techniques and the results show that DFR is superior slightly with respect to F1 score.

A novel AE-based neural network [47] is developed to determine applicable knowledge about the existing relations between the spatial and temporal attributes by integrating multiple autoencoders with recurrent CNN. Shi [48] built a deep learning-based source detection technique to determine the various video sources from an encrypted channel. Wang et al. [2] applied deep learning approaches and built a framework called Software Defined Networking—Home Gateway (SDN-HGW) for ET classification of mobile service. The core of the framework is named as DataNet, which is basically an encrypted data packet classifier deploying deep learning approaches. Three deep learning models such as Stacked autoencoder (SAE), Convolutional Neural Networks and Multilayer Perceptron (MLP) were deployed on a public dataset of over 2,00,000 encrypted data from 15 real-time applications. The maximum performance is obtained in this framework in terms of classification and computational effectiveness. Zheng et al. [49] built an architecture for identifying encrypted malicious traffic using ML. The framework uses Graph Convolutional Network (GCN) and analyses the statistical information of more than 1300 network flows. A two-phase approach is used. A feature extractor which uses an enhanced GCN is utilised in the first phase and a Decision Tree (DT) classifier in the second phase. Maximum accuracy and F1-score of more than 98% is obtained. Shuang et al. [50] classified encrypted traffic using GCN to differentiate between VPN and classified traffic into various categories such as file and emails.

Tseng et al. [51] determined malicious flow detection using HTTP headers and payloads, resulting in 93% accuracy. However, an accuracy of 99% is obtained using vanilla backpropagation. The authors used different kinds of malware families to analyse the performance.

Various DL architectures are analysed [8] using CNN and LSTM networks to accomplish ET classification. A deep learning model named MalDIST [7] is developed for ET malware classification, which produces superior results than ML and DL models. MalDIST resulted in 99.7% performance for most of the benign/malware classification metrics.

5.4   Proposed Model for Darknet Traffic Classification

Darknet is the unused address space of the Internet. The Tor network is encrypted, which ensures anonymity during web page access. Tor is not capable of protecting from all online applications. The onion routing makes the Tor slower in comparison to VPN. However, VPN can protect from all online connections. In addition, VPN is faster compared to Tor. Only 4% of the Internet constitutes the clear web and 96% is the deep web and Darknet. Figure 5.3 shows the basic working of TorNet. The data is encapsulated and sent into the encryption layers using an onion routing protocol. A series of network nodes alias onion routers peel each layer of encryption, thereby revealing the next destination of data. The data reaches the destination when the final layer is decrypted. Each intermediate node knows only the immediate node position before and after it, the sender identity is not known.

The multi-layered, fragmented and non-indexed pattern of the Darknet creates difficulty in identifying the criminals. Modern techniques are required to mitigate the potential threats in the Darknet traffic.

A machine learning-based Darknet Traffic Detection System (DTDS) is developed for IoT networks [52]. Six supervised machine learning techniques, namely,

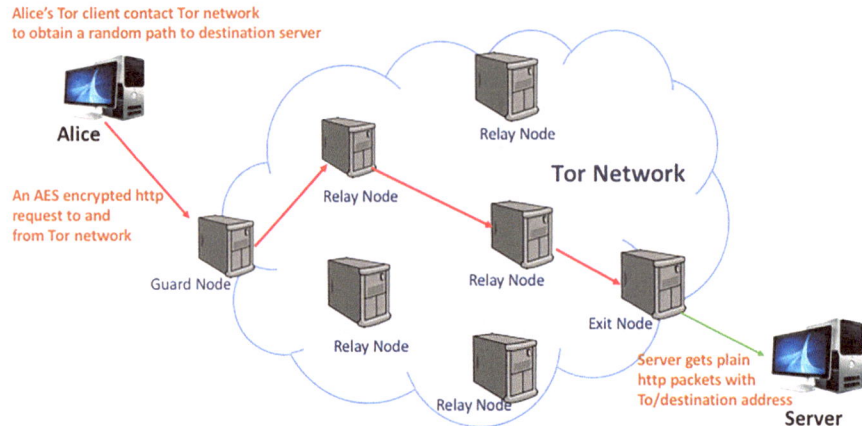

Fig. 5.3 Tor network

Table 5.6 Summary of the surveyed research works

Technique	Contribution
SVM [53]	Effective for Darknet traffic classification for TCP-based sessions
Clustering algorithms [54]	Analysing 12 clustering approaches, current concerns and recommendations for traffic flow clustering
Six machine learning approaches [55]	Differentiating VPN from non-VPN traffic and demonstrating that gradient boosting tree and random Forest are the best ML approaches
K-nearest neighbour and C4.5 decision tree (DT) [56]	Building multi-class classifiers to accurately categorise VPN and seven various classifications
DT and tri-training algorithm [57]	A hierarchical classification approach for differentiating tor anonymous traffic from other traffic

AdaBoost Decision Tree Ensemble (ADA-DT), Bagging Decision Tree Ensemble (BAG-DT), RUSBoosted Decision Tree Ensemble (RUS-DT), optimizable discriminant (O-DSC), optimizable k-nearest neighbour (O-KNN) and optimizable decision tree (OT-DT). The implemented DTDS models are evaluated on the CIC-Darknet2020 dataset. It is observed that BAG-DT performs better accuracy of 99.50% with low overhead of 9.09 microseconds. Table 5.6 summarises the survey research work on applying machine learning techniques for encrypted traffic classification. Ensemble of machine learning algorithms on CIC-Darknet2020 dataset was able to distinguish traffic. Nilesh et al. [58] analysed various models like logistic classifier, tree-based classifier, Naïve Bayes and ensemble approaches on CIC-Darknet2020 dataset. Dimensionality reduction and sampling is performed using PCA and SMOTE, respectively. Various performance metrics are evaluated and it is observed that Decision Tree and Extra Tree perform better classification resulting in maximum accuracy. Romil et al. [59] developed an approach for identifying the criminal activities in Darknet using an integration of light gradient boosting with term frequency-inverse document frequency (TF-IDF). The model resulted in an accuracy of 98.97% and had a superior result compared to other approaches. Iliadis et al. [60] utilised various common machine learning approaches to detect Darknet traffic. In the initial classification, there were two categories: "Benign" and "Darknet", while in the second there were four classes: "Tor", "Non Tor", "VPN" and "Non VPN". An average detection accuracy of 98% is obtained with the RF algorithm for both classification.

A two-layered approach is utilised in CIC-Darknet2020 dataset to generate benign and Darknet traffic in the first layer. The proposed architecture is shown in Fig. 5.4. Various preprocessing steps performed are data cleaning, encoding, sampling and normalisation. In the data cleaning phase, null values are filled with the mean of the column. The various class labels and their count in the dataset is given in Table 5.7. The non-Tor traffic is highest among all, constituting 93,356 samples, and the Tor traffic is minimal, containing 1392 in number. The dataset is hugely unbalanced in nature. Therefore, a sampling is performed to balance the data, i.e. to balance the number of each class in the label. Label Encoding is the process of converting the labels into numeric form for machine readable format. For example, the

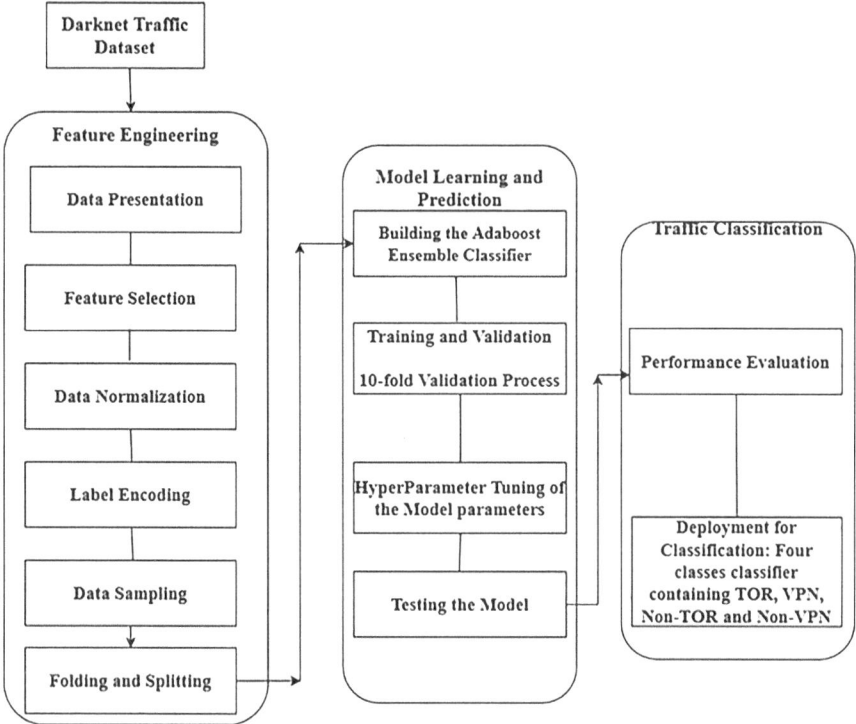

Fig. 5.4 Architecture of the proposed model

Table 5.7 Class label details after sampling on CIC-Darknet2020 dataset

Class category	No. of samples
Non-tor	23,849
Non-VPN	23,824
VPN	22,968
Tor	22,919

Table 5.8 Hyperparameter tuning using GridSearchCV

Model parameters	Best score
Learning rate: 0.05, 0.1, 0.7	0.1
n_estimators: 100, 250, 500	500
max_depth: 4, 6, 8	4

output class labels are encoded as {non-Tor represents 00, non-VPN represents 01, Tor represents 02 and VPN represents 03}.

In the final phase, the following are performed: divide data into train and test; model selection and performing hyperparameter tuning using tenfold cross-validation; obtaining the best parameters; tuning the model on best parameters on the test data. AdaBoost classifier is selected as the model.

Table 5.8 shows the hyperparameter tuning results on the AdaBoost classifier. The learning rate parameter is tuned with various values such as 0.05, 0.1 and 0.7. Similarly, max-depth is tuned with 4, 6 and 8. The final parameter such as n_estimators is tuned with 100, 250 and 500. These are the hyperparameters of AdaBoost classifier. It is inferred that "learning_rate": 0.1, "max_depth": 4 and "n_estimators": 500 are the optimal parameters. The parameters are fed for model testing and maximum performance is obtained as shown in Table 5.9.

5.5   Proposed XAI Model

A prototype for analysing encrypted network traffic is built using Explainable Machine Learning (EML) to achieve higher accuracy without any time and memory overhead. This type of model allows users to understand the classification decisions in a better manner. This kind of model is utilised to monitor the network from malware, viruses, DDoS and other similar issues. Explainable AI (XAI) is a relatively new field of machine learning that aims to discover various models" decision-making ability. The advantage of XAI is that it allows humans to interpret the machine learning model and its attributes.

Table 5.9 Performance
metrics

Metrics	Result
Accuracy	0.944
Precision	0.999
Recall	0.969
F-score	0.984

5.5.1 Background

Arnaldo et al. [61] built an interactive framework that utilises the concept of XAI to perform feature discovery to identify attacks. The three cybersecurity datasets used in this study were 1999 KDD Cup [62], a Kaggle Credit Card Dataset [63] and one curated dataset created by the authors. The authors used Principal Component Analysis to identify features which raised an anomaly detection alarm, and the research is directed to allow cybersecurity analysts to easily search for new attacks. The authors also proved that the investigation budget of anomaly detection with their method did not necessarily improve accuracy. While the principals of XAI were applied here, the application was limited to feature importance discovery. Rosenberg et al. [64] attempted to modify adversarial IDS models by including modification of existing models. The authors utilised the Ember [65] dataset and split the adversarial example generation task into two parts. First, the importance of all features is determined using XAI techniques with DeepLearn [66], and then feature-specific modification is carried out for each feature one-by-one. The authors also proved that their proposed methodology preserves the transferability and explainability of models to other similar use cases. Kinead et al. [67] focused on incorporating eXplainability into a CNN-based Android Malware Detection model proposed by McLaughlin et al. [68]. They utilised LIME to identify features of high importance and compare them to opcode sequence locations that the CNN deems malicious. However, the ultimate conclusion of this research was that the highly accurate CNN was indeed an optimal solution for malware detection.

Liu et al. [69] proposed a framework FAIXID for the eXplainability of AI-based IDS. Their main approach features Exploratory Data Analysis and Data Cleaning. They utilised popular XAI tools such as LIME and the AIX360 toolkit to create the framework. The framework was tested using the UGR'16 [70] dataset. The framework improves the data quality using data cleaning techniques. In addition, dimensionality measurements of the data are performed. Then Exploratory Data Analysis is used to analyse the data. The next module comprises the XAI techniques such as BRCG and the final module includes techniques such as CEM.

Mahbooba et al. [71] created an explainable IDS with the help of rule extraction by ID3 Decision Trees. The authors extracted the rules from the Decision Tree from the Rattle package in R [72]. The authors studied the features for information gain in the Decision Tree model. Their DT model outperformed linear regression and a linear SVM classifier and an accuracy metric is used to determine the prediction of malicious and normal attacks.

Mane et al. [73] utilised deep NNs, existing XAI toolkits and methods in order to demystify classification on the NSL-KDD dataset. LIME is used to generate local explanations for model decisions around perturbed samples. SHAP [48] measures the contribution made by each feature to the final prediction. IBM research toolkit AI EXplainability 360 (AIX360) [74] supports eight different algorithms for eXplainability, out of which ProtoDash, Boolean Decision Rules via Column Generation (BRCG) and Contrastive Explanation Method (CEM) are used to explain and summarise the dataset as well as train an interpretable model. The explanations generated by the framework are meant to validate model learning, patterns learnt by the model and the importance of features.

Rao et al. [75] attempted to use various types of XAI methods to identify attack traffic from normal data and auto-generate labels that can be presented to an analyst. The authors used an Isolation Forest binary classification approach to preliminarily perform anomaly detection which is later sent for auto-labelling. The XAI methods used for this analysis were SHAP [76], BRCG and CEM from AIX360 [77], LIME [78]. The SHAP algorithm confirms that different dependencies exist for the features for every distinct attack type. Then, the BRCG algorithm in the AIX360 is used to extract rules for anomaly detection. The automatic labels are extracted by the features that deviate for certain attack types.

Sarhan et al. [79] attempted to add eXplainability to the variation in accuracy due to feature selection techniques on common IDS datasets. CSE-CIC-IDS-2018 [80], ToN-IoT [81] and BoT-IoT [82] were the three datasets used for the study. The authors utilised Deep Feed Forward and Random Forest Classifiers for the research. SHAP [83] Analysis was carried out to identify common features amongst the three datasets that played vital roles in classification of an attack. The average SHAP values for the different datatypes were also compared for the two different classifiers.

Scalas [84] utilised eXplainable AI techniques to measure the vulnerability of the system to zero-day attacks. To this end, she has employed two synthetic measures of the explanation evenness that does not require computationally expensive attacks. The suggested technique was implemented with multiple gradient-based techniques for XAI out of which Integrated Gradients outperformed. These metrics were tested on the Debrian dataset. The work is extended into other domains of traffic analysis.

Tcydenova et al. [85] proposed an XAI-based IDS to detect adversarial attacks. Initially, a normal SVM classifier is trained on the 1999 KDD Cup [62] dataset. Then, LIME is used to extract an explanation of the non-attack records in the dataset. This is then used to identify features that are supposed to be classified as non-attack.

Wawrowski et al. [86] attempted to use XAI to identify man-made anomalies in the regSOC-KES2021 dataset. Four classification methods, namely Random Forest, NN, Logistic Regression and Gradient Boosting are used for testing the data. The intrusion detection is performed on binary class data, either attack or benign in order to identify anomalies. One random observation was selected from each attack that the models identified as anomalies. Then, the SHAP coefficient [83] was calculated for each variable that contributed to the decision. However, this model is not applicable in real-world scenarios as it requires manual identification of exact attack type. This means that the mitigation of recovery from the attack cannot be automated and cannot occur at all without a cybersecurity specialist.

5.5.2 Methodology

The model is developed using Jupyter Notebook suitable in the Anaconda environment and Google Colab. The model is tested using CSE-CIC-IDS2018 ET dataset [43]. The dataset has 80 features and 15 different attack classes: Benign, BForce, SFTP, SSH-Patator, DoS slowloris, DoSslowhttp, DoS Hulk, DoSGoldenEye, FTP-Patator, Web Attack, Infiltration, Botnet, Portscan, DDoS LOIT and SQLInject. The statistics are given in Table 5.15. The model is developed in various stages namely, Data Exploration, Control Case Model Building, EXplainability of Black Box models, XAI Specific Modelling, Comparison and Testing. The Data Exploration step involves cleaning, correlation analysis and class-imbalance discovery. This stage will not contain any main XAI functionality. The Control Case Model Building stage comprises testing the various supervised (SVM and RF) models on the cleaned dataset. This stage also includes one semi-supervised learning model (label propagation). It will also include hyperparameter tuning and preliminary feature selection. Black box models are any models that are not naturally interpretable by humans. The originally trained SVM and RF classifiers are considered as the black box classifiers. The decision-making of these models is expected to improve the functionality of future models. In the XAI Specific Modelling phase, the best performing models from the previous stage will be evaluated using XAI frameworks. The testing stage includes testing with a controlled user group to evaluate the effectiveness of model transparency using XAI. Figure 5.5 shows the methodology and framework of the Explainable AI approach. The heuristics used in this research work are as follows: The data analysis is performed using PCA (Principal Component Analysis) and correlation analysis. RF is used as ML classifier. SHAPKernels, LIME and Morris Sensitivity are used as Explainable traditional models. In addition, Explainable Boosting Machine, Decision Tree and Decision Rule list are used as explainable models. The efficiency of the Explainable Machine Learning techniques will be tested on and against a control case algorithm. The RF classifier is used as outlier identifier. The size of the dataframe is 2,830,743 rows and 79 columns.

5.5.3 Control Case Model Building

RF is a black box classifier which mostly produces accurate results despite overfitting. A zero-day classifier was also built using RF which resulted in 50% accuracy. Table 5.10 shows the performance metrics.

Table 5.15 Classification results of control case zero (after explainability)

Model	Accuracy	Classification Matrix				
			Precision	Recall	F1-Score	Support
RF	50%	0	0.50	1.00	0.67	55631
		1	0.00	0.00	0.00	55899
		Acc			0.50	111530
		Macro Avg	0.25	0.50	0.33	111530
		Weighted Avg	0.25	0.50	0.33	111530
			Precision	Recall	F1-Score	Support
LightGBM	77%	0	0.77	1.00	0.87	304971
		1	0.00	0.00	0.00	93544
		Acc			0.77	398515
		Macro Avg	0.38	0.50	0.43	398515
		Weighted Avg	0.59	0.77	0.66	398515
			Precision	Recall	F1-Score	Support
XBM	77%	0	0.77	1.00	0.87	304971
		1	1.00	0.00	0.00	93544
		Acc			0.77	398515
		Macro Avg	0.88	0.50	0.43	398515
		Weighted Avg	0.82	0.77	0.66	398515

5.5.4   Light Gradient Boosting

The results of both classification testing and zero-day testing of light gradient boost-ing classifier (LGB) were similar to that of RF—the models were overfitting the data into the benign category because the result is the same as 80% accuracy. It is given in the tables below. The eXplainability results gave the same information as for RF: it was evident that the model was not receiving enough data to make the

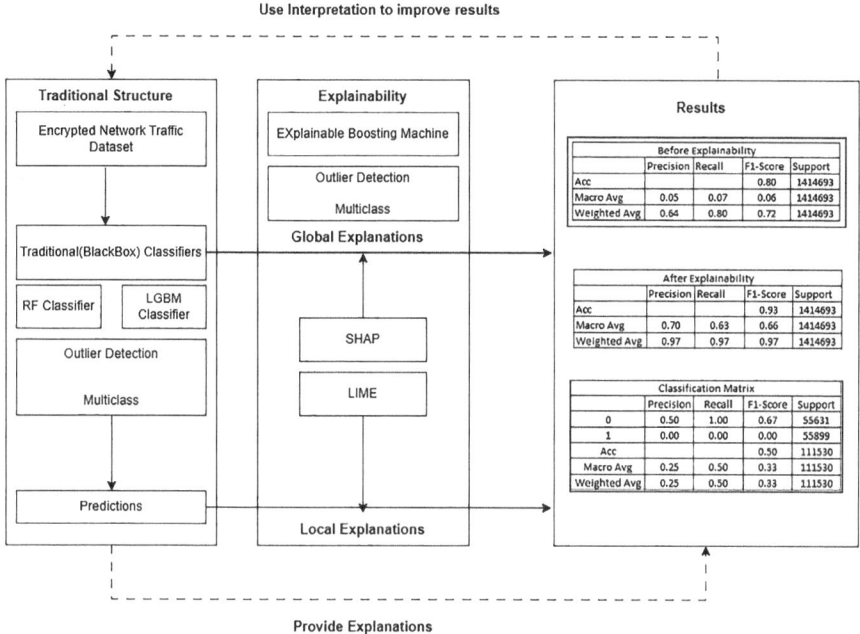

Fig. 5.5 Explainability framework

Table 5.10 Performance metrics of RF control case

	Precision	Recall	F1-score	Support
Acc			0.80	1,414,693
Macro Avg	0.05	0.07	0.06	1,414,693
Weighted Avg	0.64	0.80	0.72	1,414,693

classification. The performance metrics determined are also shown in Table 5.11. The preliminary testing of EBM as a zero-day attack analyser was trained in 137.64 s and with a test AUC of 0.500 is shown in Table 5.12. The model had nearly five features which did not contribute to the learning. Some features like BwdAvg Bulk Rate were confusing the model in prediction. According to Explainability, the features that had the highest effect are given in Table 5.13.

5.6 Discussion

A random undersampling is performed with the selected features due to the hardware constraints in the system. Therefore, the results of eXplainability are not tested on the control models. The results obtained under different conditions are shown in

Table 5.11 Performance metrics of EBM

	Precision	Recall	F1-score	Support
0	0.77	1.00	0.87	304,971
1	0.00	0.00	0.00	93,544
Acc			0.77	398,515
Macro Avg	0.38	0.50	0.43	398,515
Weighted Avg	0.59	0.77	0.66	398,515

Table 5.12 Performance metrics of EBM as a zero-day attack analyser

	Precision	Recall	F1-score	Support
0	0.77	1.00	0.87	304,971
1	1.00	0.00	0.00	93,544
Acc			0.77	398,515
Macro Avg	0.88	0.50	0.43	398,515
Weighted Avg	0.82	0.77	0.66	398,515

Table 5.13 Features selected

Features selected	Features selected
FwdAvg bytes/bulk	BwdAvg bytes/bulk
FwdAvg packets/bulk	Bwd URG flags
BwdAvg bytes/bulk	Bwd PSH flags
BwdAvg bulk rate	FwdAvg bulk rate
Fwd URG flags	CWE flag count
BwdAvg bulk rate	Label

Tables 5.14, 5.15 and 5.16, respectively. The results without feature engineering show that the EBM and light GBM have exactly the same classification accuracy. This can be attributed to similar learning techniques as both utilise Gradient Boosting Machines. However, EBM provided information about which attributes are heavily utilised and, therefore, able to apply feature engineering.

The following points are observed and the reasons for the same are described below:

- Accuracy is very low in the initial testing phase.

The real world dataset is highly imbalanced. There is little correlation between the attributes and the label. This is due to the fact that all attributes are extracted from encrypted data. This study is mainly performed because encrypted traffic is difficult to analyse. The models were not able to analyse the encrypted data initially, which caused overfitting into the majority class label "benign".

- Original run of EBM is successful.

RF and LGB are powerful ML models. EBM is a newer version with various technologies integrated into one classifier. It is important to note that the general classification was still not successful. It was merely insightful. Only the zero-day attack version was successful.

Table 5.14 Classification results of control case classification models (before explainability)

Model	Accuracy	Classification Matrix				
RF	80%		Preci sion	Recal l	F1- Score	Support
		Acc			0.80	1414693
		Macro Avg	0.05	0.07	0.06	1414693
		Weighted Avg	0.64	0.80	0.72	1414693
LightGBM	80%		Preci sion	Reca ll	F1- Score	Support
		Acc			0.80	1131754
		Macro Avg	0.05	0.07	0.06	1131754
		Weighted Avg	0.64	0.80	0.72	1131754
XBM	80%		Preci sion	Reca ll	F1- Score	Support
		Acc			0.80	1414693
		Macro Avg	0.05	0.07	0.06	1414693
		Weighted Avg	0.64	0.80	0.72	1414693

- Results improved in the proposed approach.

The primary objective in ML approach is to integrate and apply the features for prediction.

While testing the EBM, the features had the most significant effect on the EBM results.

The models were run iteratively to study the results and determine which features are to be retained and removed. At the end, an optimal feature set is obtained.

5.7 Conclusion

In this chapter, various machine learning and deep learning-based encrypted traffic analysis are discussed in detail. Two models are explained in this chapter. The first model detects Darknet traffic using the AdaBoost classifier on CIC-Darknet2020

Table 5.16 Comparison of EBM results before and after explainability

Test Case	Before Explainability				After Explainability			
EBM atack classifier Classification Matrix		Precision	Recall	F1-Score	Support		Precision	Recall	F1-Score	Support

EBM atack classifier Classification Matrix — Before Explainability:

	Precision	Recall	F1-Score	Support
Acc			0.80	1414693
Macro Avg	.05	0.07	0.06	1414693
Weighted Avg	.64	0.80	0.72	1414693

EBM atack classifier Classification Matrix — After Explainability:

	Precision	Recall	F1-Score	Support
Acc			0.93	1414693
Macro Avg	0.70	0.63	0.66	1414693
Weighted Avg	0.97	0.97	0.97	1414693

EBM attack classifier Accuracy	80%	93%

EBM zero-day classifier Classification Matrix — Before Explainability:

	Precision	Recall	F1-Score	Support
0	0.77	1.00	0.87	304971
1	1.00	0.00	0.00	93544
Acc			0.77	398515
Macro Avg	0.88	0.50	0.43	398515
Weighted Avg	0.82	0.77	0.66	398515

EBM zero-day classifier Classification Matrix — After Explainability:

	Precision	Recall	F1-Score	Support
0	0.99	1.00	0.99	304971
1	1.00	0.98	0.99	93544
Acc			0.99	398515
Macro Avg	1.00	0.99	0.99	398515
Weighted Avg	0.99	1.00	0.99	

EBM zero-day classifier accuracy	77%	99%

dataset. Experimental Analysis shows superior performance on accuracy, precision, recall and F-score. The second model is Explainable Boosting Machine (EBM) using Explainable Artificial Intelligence (XAI) to classify the encrypted traffic of CSE-CIC-IDS2018 dataset. The results show that EBM outperformed other models like Random Forest (RF) and Light Gradient Boosting (LGB).

References

1. Google Transparency Report. (n.d.). Retrieved April 28, 2021, from https://transparencyreport. google.com/https/overview?hl=en
2. Wang, P., Ye, F., Chen, X., & Qian, Y. (2018). Datanet: Deep learning based encrypted network traffic classification in SDN home gateway. *IEEE Access, 6*, 55380–55391.
3. Hu, X., Gu, C., & Wei, F. (2021). CLD-net: A network combining CNN and LSTM for internet encrypted traffic classification. *Security and Communication Networks, 2021*, 1–15.
4. Alshammari, R., & Zincir-Heywood, A. N. (2007). A flow based approach for SSH traffic detection. In *2007 IEEE international conference on systems, man and cybernetics* (pp. 296–301). IEEE.
5. Sommer, R., & Paxson, V. (2010). Outside the closed world: On using machine learning for network intrusion detection. In *2010 IEEE symposium on security and privacy* (pp. 305–316). IEEE.
6. Moore, A., Zuev, D., & Crogan, M. (2013). *Discriminators for use in flow-based classification*.
7. Bader, O., Lichy, A., Hajaj, C., Dubin, R., & Dvir, A. (2022). MalDIST: From encrypted traffic classification to malware traffic detection and classification. In *2022 IEEE 19th annual consumer communications & networking conference (CCNC)* (pp. 527–533). IEEE.
8. Lopez-Martin, M., Carro, B., Sanchez-Esguevillas, A., & Lloret, J. (2017). Network traffic classifier with convolutional and recurrent neural networks for internet of things. *IEEE Access, 5*, 18042–18050.
9. Fu, Y., Xiong, H., Lu, X., Yang, J., & Chen, C. (2016). Service usage classification with encrypted internet traffic in mobile messaging apps. *IEEE Transactions on Mobile Computing, 15*(11), 2851–2864.
10. Yao, Z., Ge, J., Wu, Y., Lin, X., He, R., & Ma, Y. (2020). Encrypted traffic classification based on Gaussian mixture models and hidden Markov models. *Journal of Network and Computer Applications, 166*, 102711.
11. Aceto, G., Ciuonzo, D., Montieri, A., & Pescapé, A. (2021). DISTILLER: Encrypted traffic classification via multimodal multitask deep learning. *Journal of Network and Computer Applications, 183*, 102985.
12. Williams, N., Zander, S., & Armitage, G. (2006). A preliminary performance comparison of five machine learning algorithms for practical IP traffic flow classification. *ACM SIGCOMM Computer Communication Review, 36*(5), 5–16.
13. Berrueta, E., Morato, D., Magaña, E., & Izal, M. (2022). Crypto-ransomware detection using machine learning models in file-sharing network scenarios with encrypted traffic. *Expert Systems with Applications, 209*, 118299.
14. Lu, G., Zhang, H., Qassrawi, M., & Yu, X. (2012). Comparison and analysis of flow features at the packet level for traffic classification. In *2012 international conference on connected vehicles and expo (ICCVE)* (pp. 262–267). IEEE.
15. Zhongsheng, W., Jianguo, W., Sen, Y., & Jiaqiong, G. (2020). Retracted: Traffic identification and traffic analysis based on support vector machine. *Concurrency and Computation: Practice and Experience, 32*(2), e5292.

16. Anthi, E., Williams, L., Słowińska, M., Theodorakopoulos, G., & Burnap, P. (2019). A supervised intrusion detection system for smart home IoT devices. *IEEE Internet of Things Journal, 6*(5), 9042–9053.

17. Arndt, D. J., & Zincir-Heywood, A. N. (2011). A comparison of three machine learning techniques for encrypted network traffic analysis. In *2011 IEEE symposium on computational intelligence for security and defense applications (CISDA)* (pp. 107–114). IEEE.

18. Canavese, D., Regano, L., Basile, C., Ciravegna, G., & Lioy, A. (2022). Encryption-agnostic classifiers of traffic originators and their application to anomaly detection. *Computers & Electrical Engineering, 97*, 107621.

19. Singh, S. K., & Roy, P. K. (2022). Malicious traffic detection of DNS over https using ensemble machine learning. *International Journal of Computing and Digital Systems, 11*(1), 189–197.

20. Abbasi, M., Shahraki, A., & Taherkordi, A. (2021). Deep learning for network traffic monitoring and analysis (NTMA): A survey. *Computer Communications, 170*, 19–41.

21. Rezaei, S., & Liu, X. (2019). Deep learning for encrypted traffic classification: An overview. *IEEE Communications Magazine, 57*(5), 76–81.

22. Zou, S., Zhong, F., Han, B., Sun, H., Qian, T., Yu, C., & Jia, J. (2021). Network intrusion detection method based on deep learning. *Journal of Physics: Conference Series, 1966*(1), 012051.

23. LeCun, Y., Bengio, Y., & Hinton, G. (2015). Deep learning. *Nature, 521*(7553), 436–444.

24. Shapira, T., & Shavitt, Y. (2019). Flowpic: Encrypted internet traffic classification is as easy as image recognition. In *IEEE INFOCOM 2019-IEEE conference on computer communications workshops (INFOCOM WKSHPS)* (pp. 680–687). IEEE.

25. Wu, Y., Wei, D., & Feng, J. (2020). Network attacks detection methods based on deep learning techniques: A survey. *Security and Communication Networks, 2020*, 1–17.

26. Wang, P., Chen, X., Ye, F., & Sun, Z. (2019). A survey of techniques for mobile service encrypted traffic classification using deep learning. *IEEE Access, 7*, 54024–54033.

27. Wang, Z. (2015). The applications of deep learning on traffic identification. *BlackHat USA, 24*(11), 1–10.

28. Lotfollahi, M., Jafari Siavoshani, M., Shirali Hossein Zade, R., & Saberian, M. (2020). Deep packet: A novel approach for encrypted traffic classification using deep learning. *Soft Computing, 24*(3), 1999–2012.

29. Wang, W., Zhu, M., Zeng, X., Ye, X., & Sheng, Y. (2017). Malware traffic classification using convolutional neural network for representation learning. In *2017 international conference on information networking (ICOIN)* (pp. 712–717). IEEE.

30. Wang, W., Zhu, M., Wang, J., Zeng, X., & Yang, Z. (2017). End-to-end encrypted traffic classification with one-dimensional convolution neural networks. In *2017 IEEE international conference on intelligence and security informatics (ISI)* (pp. 43–48). IEEE.

31. Aceto, G., Ciuonzo, D., Montieri, A., & Pescapé, A. (2018). Mobile encrypted traffic classification using deep learning. In *2018 network traffic measurement and analysis conference (TMA)* (pp. 1–8). IEEE.

32. Tong, V., Tran, H. A., Souihi, S., & Mellouk, A. (2018). A novel QUIC traffic classifier based on convolutional neural networks. In *2018 IEEE global communications conference (GLOBECOM)* (pp. 1–6). IEEE.

33. Chen, Z., He, K., Li, J., & Geng, Y. (2017). Seq2img: A sequence-to-image based approach towards IP traffic classification using convolutional neural networks. In *2017 IEEE International conference on big data (big data)* (pp. 1271–1276). IEEE.

34. Goyal, P., & Goyal, A. (2017). Comparative study of two most popular packet sniffing tools-Tcpdump and Wireshark. In *2017 9th international conference on computational intelligence and communication networks (CICN)* (pp. 77–81). IEEE.

35. Hofstede, R., Čeleda, P., Trammell, B., Drago, I., Sadre, R., Sperotto, A., & Pras, A. (2014). Flow monitoring explained: From packet capture to data analysis with netflow and ipfix. *IEEE Communications Surveys & Tutorials, 16*(4), 2037–2064.

36. Gil, G. D., Lashkari, A. H., Mamun, M., & Ghorbani, A. A. (2016). Characterization of encrypted and VPN traffic using time-related features. In *Proceedings of the 2nd interna-*

tional conference on information systems security and privacy (ICISSP 2016) (pp. 407–414). SciTePress.

37. Li, D., Zhu, Y., & Lin, W. (2017). Traffic identification of mobile apps based on variational autoencoder network. In *2017 13th international conference on computational intelligence and security (CIS)* (pp. 287–291). IEEE.

38. Zhang, H., Wu, C. Q., Gao, S., Wang, Z., Xu, Y., & Liu, Y. (2018). An effective deep learning based scheme for network intrusion detection. In *2018 24th international conference on pattern recognition (ICPR)* (pp. 682–687). IEEE.

39. Aygun, R. C., & Yavuz, A. G. (2017). Network anomaly detection with stochastically improved autoencoder based models. In *2017 IEEE 4th international conference on cyber security and cloud computing (CSCloud)* (pp. 193–198). IEEE.

40. Lee, H., Han, S., & Lee, J. (2017). Generative adversarial trainer: Defense to adversarial perturbations with gan. *arXiv preprint arXiv:1705.03387.*

41. Vu, L., Bui, C. T., & Nguyen, Q. U. (2017). A deep learning based method for handling imbalanced problem in network traffic classification. In *Proceedings of the 8th international symposium on information and communication technology* (pp. 333–339).

42. Lin, Z., Shi, Y., & Xue, Z. (2022). Idsgan: Generative adversarial networks for attack generation against intrusion detection. In *Pacific-Asia conference on knowledge discovery and data mining* (pp. 79–91). Springer International Publishing.

43. Liu, X., You, J., Wu, Y., Li, T., Li, L., Zhang, Z., & Ge, J. (2020). Attention-based bidirectional GRU networks for efficient HTTPS traffic classification. *Information Sciences, 541,* 297–315.

44. Liu, C., He, L., Xiong, G., Cao, Z., & Li, Z. (2019). Fs-net: A flow sequence network for encrypted traffic classification. In *IEEE INFOCOM 2019-IEEE conference on computer communications* (pp. 1171–1179). IEEE.

45. Cheng, J., Wu, Y., Yuepeng, E., You, J., Li, T., Li, H., & Ge, J. (2021). MATEC: A lightweight neural network for online encrypted traffic classification. *Computer Networks, 199,* 108472.

46. Zeng, Y., Gu, H., Wei, W., & Guo, Y. (2019). $ deep-full-range $: A deep learning based network encrypted traffic classification and intrusion detection framework. *IEEE Access, 7,* 45182–45190.

47. D'Angelo, G., & Palmieri, F. (2021). Network traffic classification using deep convolutional recurrent autoencoder neural networks for spatial–temporal features extraction. *Journal of Network and Computer Applications, 173,* 102890.

48. Shi, Y., Feng, D., Cheng, Y., & Biswas, S. (2021). A natural language-inspired multilabel video streaming source identification method based on deep neural networks. *Signal, Image and Video Processing, 15*(6), 1161–1168.

49. Zheng, J., Zeng, Z., & Feng, T. (2022). GCN-ETA: High-efficiency encrypted malicious traffic detection. *Security and Communication Networks, 2022,* 1–11.

50. Mo, S., Wang, Y., Xiao, D., Wu, W., Fan, S., & Shi, C. (2020). Encrypted traffic classification using graph convolutional networks. In *Advanced data mining and applications: 16th international conference, ADMA 2020, Foshan, China, November 12–14, 2020, Proceedings 16* (pp. 207–219). Springer International Publishing.

51. Tseng, A., Chen, Y., Kao, Y., & Lin, T. (2016). Deep learning for ransomware detection. *IEICE Technical Report, 116*(282), 87–92.

52. Abu Al-Haija, Q., Krichen, M., & Abu Elhaija, W. (2022). Machine-learning-based darknet traffic detection system for IoT applications. *Electronics, 11*(4), 556.

53. Turkett, W. H., Jr., Karode, A. V., & Fulp, E. W. (2008). In-the-dark network traffic classification using support vector machines. *AAAI, 3,* 1745–1750.

54. Erman, J., Arlitt, M., & Mahanti, A. (2006). Traffic classification using clustering algorithms. In *Proceedings of the 2006 SIGCOMM workshop on mining network data* (pp. 281–286).

55. Bagui, S., Fang, X., Kalaimannan, E., Bagui, S. C., & Sheehan, J. (2017). Comparison of machine-learning algorithms for classification of VPN network traffic flow using time-related features. *Journal of Cyber Security Technology, 1*(2), 108–126.

56. Draper-Gil, G., Lashkari, A. H., Mamun, M. S. I., & Ghorbani, A. A. (2016). Characterization of encrypted and VPN traffic using time-related. In *Proceedings of the 2nd international conference on information systems security and privacy (ICISSP)* (pp. 407–414).

57. Lingyu, J., Yang, L., Bailing, W., Hongri, L., & Guodong, X. (2017). A hierarchical classification approach for tor anonymous traffic. In *2017 IEEE 9th international conference on communication software and networks (ICCSN)* (pp. 239–243). IEEE.

58. Jadav, N., Dutta, N., Sarma, H. K. D., Pricop, E., & Tanwar, S. (2021). A machine learning approach to classify network traffic. In *2021 13th international conference on electronics, computers and artificial intelligence (ECAI)* (pp. 1–6). IEEE.

59. Rawat, R., Mahor, V., Chirgaiya, S., Shaw, R. N., & Ghosh, A. (2021). Analysis of darknet traffic for criminal activities detection using TF-IDF and light gradient boosted machine learning algorithm. In *Innovations in electrical and electronic engineering: Proceedings of ICEEE 2021* (pp. 671–681). Springer Singapore.

60. Iliadis, L. A., & Kaifas, T. (2021). Darknet traffic classification using machine learning techniques. In *2021 10th international conference on modern circuits and systems technologies (MOCAST)* (pp. 1–4). IEEE.

61. Arnaldo, I., Veeramachaneni, K., & Lam, M. (2019). eX2: A framework for interactive anomaly detection. In *IUI Workshops*.

62. UCI, KDD. *The third international knowledge discovery and data mining tools competition dataset KDD Cup 1999 data.* http://kdd.ics.uci.edu/databases/kddcup99/kddcup.

63. Machine Learning Group ULB, "Credit Card Fraud Detection," Kaggle, 2017. [Online]. Available: https://www.kaggle.com/mlg-ulb/creditcardfraud.

64. Rosenberg, I., Meir, S., Berrebi, J., Gordon, I., Sicard, G., & David, E. O. (2020). Generating end-to-end adversarial examples for malware classifiers using explainability. In *2020 international joint conference on neural networks (IJCNN)* (pp. 1–10). IEEE.

65. Anderson, H. S., & Roth, P. (2018). Ember: An open dataset for training static pe malware machine learning models. *arXiv preprint arXiv:1804.04637.*

66. Ancona, M., Ceolini, E., Öztireli, C., & Gross, M. (2017). Towards better understanding of gradient-based attribution methods for deep neural networks. *arXiv preprint arXiv:1711.06104.*

67. Kinkead, M., Millar, S., McLaughlin, N., & O'Kane, P. (2021). Towards explainable CNNs for Android malware detection. *Procedia Computer Science, 184*, 959–965.

68. McLaughlin, N., Martinez del Rincon, J., Kang, B., Yerima, S., Miller, P., Sezer, S., Safaei, Y., Trickel, E., Zhao, Z., Doupé, A., & Joon Ahn, G. (2017). Deep android malware detection. In *Proceedings of the seventh ACM on conference on data and application security and privacy* (pp. 301–308).

69. Liu, H., Zhong, C., Alnusair, A., & Islam, S. R. (2021). FAIXID: A framework for enhancing ai explainability of intrusion detection results using data cleaning techniques. *Journal of Network and Systems Management, 29*(4), 40.

70. Maciá-Fernández, G., Camacho, J., Magán-Carrión, R., García-Teodoro, P., & Therón, R. (2018). UGR'16: A new dataset for the evaluation of cyclostationarity-based network IDSs. *Computers & Security, 73*, 411–424.

71. Mahbooba, B., Timilsina, M., Sahal, R., & Serrano, M. (2021). Explainable artificial intelligence (XAI) to enhance trust management in intrusion detection systems using decision tree model. *Complexity, 2021*, 1–11.

72. Williams, G. (2011). *Data mining with rattle and R: The art of excavating data for knowledge discovery.* Springer Science & Business Media.

73. Mane, S., & Rao, D. (2021). Explaining network intrusion detection system using explainable AI framework. *arXiv preprint arXiv:2103.07110.*

74. IBM, "AIX360," Linux Foundation AI & Data, [Online]. Available: https://aix360.mybluemix.net/. Accessed 2021.

75. Rao, D., & Mane, S. (2021). Zero-shot learning approach to adaptive cybersecurity using explainable AI. *arXiv preprint arXiv:2106.14647.*

76. Spinner, T., Schlegel, U., Schäfer, H., & El-Assady, M. (2019). explAIner: A visual analytics framework for interactive and explainable machine learning. *IEEE Transactions on Visualization and Computer Graphics, 26*(1), 1064–1074.

77. Burkart, N., & Huber, M. F. (2021). A survey on the explainability of supervised machine learning. *Journal of Artificial Intelligence Research, 70*, 245–317.

78. Samek, W., Montavon, G., Vedaldi, A., Hansen, L. K., & Müller, K. R. (Eds.). (2019). *Explainable AI: Interpreting, explaining and visualizing deep learning* (Vol. 11700). Springer Nature.

79. Sarhan, M., Layeghy, S., & Portmann, M. (2022). Evaluating standard feature sets towards increased generalisability and explainability of ML-based network intrusion detection. *Big Data Research, 30*, 100359.

80. Sharafaldin, I., Lashkari, A. H., & Ghorbani, A. A. (2018). Toward generating a new intrusion detection dataset and intrusion traffic characterization. *ICISSp, 1*, 108–116.

81. Moustafa, N. (2019). *ToN_IoT datasets*. IEEE Dataport.

82. Koroniotis, N., Moustafa, N., Sitnikova, E., & Turnbull, B. (2019). Towards the development of realistic botnet dataset in the internet of things for network forensic analytics: Bot-IOT dataset. *Future Generation Computer Systems, 100*, 779–796.

83. Lundberg, S. M., & Lee, S. I. (2017). A unified approach to interpreting model predictions. *Advances in Neural Information Processing Systems, 30*.

84. Scalas, M. (2021). *Malware analysis and detection with explainable machine learning*.

85. Choi, I., Lee, J., Kwon, T., Kim, K., Choi, Y., & Song, J. (2021). An easy-to-use framework to build and operate AI-based intrusion detection for in-situ monitoring. In *2021 16th Asia joint conference on information security (AsiaJCIS)* (pp. 1–8). IEEE.

86. Wawrowski, Ł., Michalak, M., Białas, A., Kurianowicz, R., Sikora, M., Uchroński, M., & Kajzer, A. (2021). Detecting anomalies and attacks in network traffic monitoring with classification methods and XAI-based explainability. *Procedia Computer Science, 192*, 2259–2268.